TYPESCRIPT PROGRAMMING IN ACTION

CODE EDITING FOR SOFTWARE ENGINEERS

4 BOOKS IN 1

BOOK 1
TYPESCRIPT FOR BEGINNERS: A STEP-BY-STEP GUIDE TO LEARNING
TYPESCRIPT PROGRAMMING

BOOK 2
MASTERING TYPESCRIPT ESSENTIALS: ADVANCED CONCEPTS AND
PRACTICAL APPLICATIONS FOR INTERMEDIATE DEVELOPERS

BOOK 3
TYPESCRIPT IN DEPTH: BUILDING WEB APPLICATIONS: EXPLORING
TYPESCRIPT WITH REAL-WORLD WEB DEVELOPMENT PROJECTS

BOOK 4
TYPESCRIPT MASTERY: EXPERT-LEVEL TECHNIQUES: OPTIMIZING
PERFORMANCE AND CRAFTING COMPLEX APPLICATIONS

ROB BOTWRIGHT

Published by Rob Botwright
Library of Congress Cataloging-in-Publication Data
ISBN 978-1-83938-671-8
Cover design by Rizzo

Disclaimer

The contents of this book are based on extensive research and the best available historical sources. However, the author and publisher make no claims, promises, or guarantees about the accuracy, completeness, or adequacy of the information contained herein. The information in this book is provided on an "as is" basis, and the author and publisher disclaim any and all liability for any errors, omissions, or inaccuracies in the information or for any actions taken in reliance on such information. The opinions and views expressed in this book are those of the author and do not necessarily reflect the official policy or position of any organization or individual mentioned in this book. Any reference to specific people, places, or events is intended only to provide historical context and is not intended to defame or malign any group, individual, or entity. The information in this book is intended for educational and entertainment purposes only. It is not intended to be a substitute for professional advice or judgment. Readers are encouraged to conduct their own research and to seek professional advice where appropriate. Every effort has been made to obtain necessary permissions and acknowledgments for all images and other copyrighted material used in this book. Any errors or omissions in this regard are unintentional, and the author and publisher will correct them in future editions.

Introduction

Welcome to "TypeScript Programming in Action: Code Editing for Software Engineers." This book bundle is a comprehensive and dynamic exploration of TypeScript, one of the most powerful and versatile programming languages in the world of web development.

In today's software landscape, the demand for skilled TypeScript developers is on the rise. TypeScript offers a robust type system, improved code quality, and enhanced developer productivity, making it a go-to choice for building modern web applications. Whether you're a beginner taking your first steps in programming or an experienced developer seeking to master TypeScript's intricacies, this bundle is designed to guide you through a transformative learning journey.

This four-volume bundle is carefully crafted to cater to a wide spectrum of readers, from those new to TypeScript to intermediate developers looking to strengthen their skills and even experts seeking advanced techniques. Let's take a closer look at what each book has to offer:

Book 1 - TypeScript for Beginners: A Step-by-Step Guide to Learning TypeScript Programming In this introductory volume, we start from the very basics, assuming no prior knowledge of TypeScript. We provide a gentle and structured approach to learning, covering fundamental concepts, data types, variables, and essential programming constructs. By the end of this book, you'll have a solid foundation in TypeScript and be ready to tackle more complex challenges.

Book 2 - Mastering TypeScript Essentials: Advanced Concepts and Practical Applications for Intermediate Developers Building on the knowledge acquired in the first book, this volume takes you deeper into TypeScript's intricacies. We explore advanced concepts, such as complex data structures, asynchronous programming, and real-world practical applications. This book is tailored for intermediate developers looking to elevate their TypeScript skills to the next level.

Book 3 - TypeScript in Depth: Building Web Applications - Exploring TypeScript with Real-World Web Development Projects In the third book, we dive into the heart of web development with TypeScript. Through a series of hands-on projects and real-world examples, we build dynamic web applications from the ground up. You'll learn how to harness TypeScript's capabilities to solve real-world problems and gain a comprehensive understanding of web development with TypeScript.

Book 4 - TypeScript Mastery: Expert-Level Techniques - Optimizing Performance and Crafting Complex Applications In the final volume, we reach the pinnacle of TypeScript expertise. This book is designed for developers seeking to become TypeScript masters. We explore expert-level techniques, including metaprogramming, dependency injection, advanced design patterns, and performance optimization. By the end of this book, you'll be equipped to tackle the most complex software development challenges with confidence.

Throughout this bundle, our focus is on practicality and real-world application. Each book is filled with code examples, best practices, and valuable insights derived from years of industry experience. Whether you're building web applications, optimizing performance, or crafting intricate software solutions, this bundle provides the knowledge and tools needed to excel in TypeScript programming.

We invite you to embark on this exciting journey through TypeScript's dynamic world. Whether you're a beginner taking your first steps or a seasoned developer striving for mastery, "TypeScript Programming in Action: Code Editing for Software Engineers" is your comprehensive guide to becoming a proficient TypeScript developer.

Let's dive in and explore the power and potential of TypeScript together. Your journey to TypeScript excellence begins here.

BOOK 1
TYPESCRIPT FOR BEGINNERS
A STEP-BY-STEP GUIDE TO LEARNING TYPESCRIPT
PROGRAMMING

ROB BOTWRIGHT

Chapter 1: Introduction to TypeScript

TypeScript is a powerful, open-source programming language that has gained popularity among developers worldwide. Developed and maintained by Microsoft, TypeScript is often regarded as a superset of JavaScript, which means it builds upon JavaScript's syntax and capabilities while adding static typing to the mix. With TypeScript, developers can write cleaner, more maintainable code, catch errors early in the development process, and enhance code quality and productivity. TypeScript's static type system enables developers to define the data types of variables, parameters, and return values explicitly, which helps in reducing runtime errors and making the codebase more self-documenting.

One of TypeScript's core features is its static type checking, which occurs at compile time, providing immediate feedback to developers about potential issues in their code. This feature allows for safer refactoring, code navigation, and better tooling support. TypeScript's type system includes primitives such as numbers, strings, booleans, and more, as well as more complex types like arrays, objects, and custom-defined types, providing a wide range of flexibility and expressiveness.

Developers can install TypeScript globally on their machines using npm, a popular package manager for

Node.js, with a simple CLI command: **npm install -g typescript**. Once installed, they can create TypeScript files with a **.ts** extension, and the TypeScript compiler, **tsc**, can be used to transpile these files into JavaScript for execution in browsers or Node.js environments. TypeScript's tooling support extends to popular integrated development environments (IDEs) such as Visual Studio Code, making it easy to write and maintain TypeScript code efficiently.

TypeScript offers support for modern JavaScript features, including ES6 and beyond, and can generate ES3, ES5, or ES6 JavaScript code depending on the developer's target environment. This adaptability ensures that TypeScript can be used in a wide range of projects, from legacy applications to cutting-edge web and mobile development.

One of TypeScript's key advantages is its ability to improve collaboration among developers. By providing clear type annotations, TypeScript makes codebases more understandable, allowing team members to work together more effectively. Additionally, TypeScript's tooling support enhances code navigation, enabling developers to explore and understand large codebases quickly.

TypeScript also offers a powerful feature known as "Declaration Files" (**.d.ts**), which allows developers to describe the shape and type of external libraries and modules in their projects. This feature ensures that TypeScript can be used with existing JavaScript libraries, making it a versatile choice for both new and established projects.

The TypeScript community is vibrant and active, with a rich ecosystem of open-source libraries and frameworks that extend its capabilities. TypeScript's compatibility with popular libraries and frameworks, such as React, Angular, and Vue.js, makes it a popular choice for front-end development. On the server side, TypeScript is used with Node.js, Express.js, and other backend technologies to create robust and scalable applications.

Developers can take advantage of TypeScript's support for asynchronous programming using promises and async/await syntax, enabling them to write cleaner and more readable code for handling asynchronous operations. This feature is especially valuable when working with network requests, file I/O, or other time-consuming tasks.

In addition to enhancing the development experience, TypeScript also contributes to better code quality and maintainability. Its static type system catches type-related errors early in the development process, reducing the likelihood of runtime errors and improving overall code reliability. This leads to more predictable behavior and fewer unexpected issues in production.

TypeScript's integration with build tools and bundlers, such as Webpack or Parcel, streamlines the development workflow and optimizes the production-ready code bundle. This integration ensures that

TypeScript projects can be efficiently built and deployed to various platforms.

To deploy a TypeScript application, developers typically follow a series of steps. First, they write their TypeScript code in **.ts** files, ensuring that type annotations are used appropriately to provide type information. Then, they transpile the TypeScript code into JavaScript using the TypeScript compiler (**tsc**). This step generates JavaScript files (**.js**) that can be executed in the desired environment.

To run the application locally, developers can use Node.js to execute the generated JavaScript files. For web applications, they may set up a development server to serve the application to a web browser.

Deployment to production typically involves additional steps, such as minifying and optimizing the JavaScript code, bundling dependencies, and configuring server hosting. These steps vary depending on the specific deployment target, whether it's a web server, a cloud platform, or a mobile app store.

In summary, TypeScript offers numerous benefits to developers, including enhanced code quality, better tooling support, and improved collaboration. Its static type system, modern JavaScript support, and ecosystem of libraries and frameworks make it a compelling choice for web and application development. By following best practices and leveraging TypeScript's capabilities, developers can create efficient, maintainable, and reliable software solutions for a wide range of projects.

The advantages of using TypeScript in modern software development are numerous and have contributed to its growing popularity among developers. TypeScript, an open-source programming language developed by Microsoft, builds upon the foundation of JavaScript while introducing several key features that enhance the development experience and code quality.

One of the primary advantages of TypeScript is its ability to catch errors at compile time through its strong static type system. Unlike JavaScript, where type errors might only surface at runtime, TypeScript allows developers to define types for variables, parameters, and return values, providing early feedback on potential issues in the code. This early error detection can lead to more robust and reliable software, reducing the likelihood of runtime errors and debugging efforts.

The TypeScript compiler, often invoked using the **tsc** command in the Command Line Interface (CLI), enforces these type annotations and transpiles TypeScript code into plain JavaScript, which can be executed in browsers or Node.js environments. This process ensures that type-related errors are addressed before the code reaches production, leading to smoother development workflows and improved code quality.

TypeScript's static type system also enhances code readability and maintainability. By explicitly defining types, developers create self-documenting code that is more accessible to other team members. This increased code clarity facilitates collaboration and makes it easier for developers to understand and modify existing codebases. Additionally, modern Integrated Development Environments (IDEs), such as Visual Studio Code, offer strong TypeScript support, providing features like intelligent code completion and real-time error checking, further improving developer productivity.

Another significant advantage of TypeScript is its compatibility with modern JavaScript features and standards. TypeScript supports the latest ECMAScript (ES) standards, allowing developers to take advantage of ES6, ES7, and beyond while writing TypeScript code. This means that TypeScript can be used in projects that require the latest JavaScript language features, ensuring that developers remain up to date with industry best practices.

TypeScript's adaptability to different JavaScript target environments is another strength. Developers can configure the TypeScript compiler to generate ES3, ES5, or ES6 code, depending on their specific project requirements and target platforms. This flexibility makes TypeScript suitable for a wide range of applications, from older legacy systems to cutting-edge web and mobile development.

Moreover, TypeScript's strong typing system extends to external libraries and modules through the use of declaration files (**.d.ts**). These declaration files describe the shape and types of third-party libraries, ensuring that TypeScript can seamlessly integrate with existing JavaScript codebases and libraries. This capability simplifies the adoption of TypeScript in projects with established codebases.

In terms of tooling and ecosystem, TypeScript benefits from a vibrant community and a rich set of open-source libraries and frameworks. Developers can leverage TypeScript in popular front-end libraries like React, Angular, and Vue.js, enhancing their ability to build scalable and maintainable web applications. On the server side, TypeScript is commonly used with Node.js, Express.js, and other backend technologies, providing a unified development experience across the full stack.

TypeScript also excels in asynchronous programming, offering robust support for promises and async/await syntax. Developers can write cleaner and more readable code when dealing with asynchronous operations, such as network requests or file I/O, making it easier to manage complex workflows.

To deploy a TypeScript application, developers follow a series of steps. First, they write their TypeScript code in **.ts** files, using type annotations to provide type information. Then, they transpile the TypeScript code into JavaScript using the TypeScript compiler (**tsc**), which generates JavaScript files (**.js**) for execution in the desired environment.

For local execution, developers can use Node.js to run the generated JavaScript files. To serve a TypeScript-based web application locally, they may set up a development server using tools like Webpack or Parcel.

Deploying to production typically involves additional steps, such as optimizing and minifying the JavaScript code, bundling dependencies, and configuring hosting. These steps vary depending on the deployment target, whether it's a web server, a cloud platform, or a mobile app store.

In summary, the advantages of using TypeScript in modern software development are clear and compelling. Its strong static typing system catches errors early, improving code quality and reliability. TypeScript enhances code readability and maintainability, making it an excellent choice for collaborative projects. Its compatibility with modern JavaScript features and ecosystems, along with its ability to target various environments, makes it versatile and adaptable. By embracing TypeScript and following best practices, developers can build robust, maintainable, and efficient software solutions.

Chapter 2: Setting Up Your Development Environment

To begin our exploration of installing Node.js and npm, it's essential to understand that Node.js is a runtime environment for executing JavaScript code on the server side, while npm stands for Node Package Manager, a powerful tool for managing and distributing JavaScript packages and libraries.

Node.js and npm are integral components of modern web development, allowing developers to build server-side applications, create command-line tools, and manage project dependencies efficiently. To get started, we'll guide you through the installation process for both Node.js and npm on various operating systems.

If you are using a Windows operating system, you can visit the official Node.js website (https://nodejs.org/) to download the Windows Installer. This installer includes both Node.js and npm. Once downloaded, run the installer and follow the on-screen instructions to complete the installation.

On macOS, you have a few installation options. You can use the official macOS Installer package available on the Node.js website, or you can use a package manager like Homebrew. To use Homebrew, open your Terminal and run the following commands:
sqlCopy code

brew update brew install node

These commands will install Node.js and npm on your macOS system.

For Linux users, the installation process may vary slightly depending on your distribution. However, you can often use a package manager to install Node.js and npm easily. For example, on Debian or Ubuntu-based systems, you can use the following commands:

sqlCopy code

sudo apt update sudo apt install nodejs npm

On Red Hat or CentOS-based systems, you can use the following commands:

arduinoCopy code

sudo yum install epel-release sudo yum install nodejs npm

Once the installation is complete, you can verify that Node.js and npm are correctly installed by opening your terminal and running the following commands:

Copy code

node -v npm -v

These commands will display the installed versions of Node.js and npm.

Now that you have Node.js and npm installed on your system, you can start using them to develop and manage JavaScript applications. Node.js allows you to run JavaScript code outside of a web browser, which is particularly useful for server-side programming. You can create Node.js applications by writing JavaScript files with a **.js** extension and executing them using the **node** command followed by the file name.

For example, if you create a file named **hello.js** with the following content:

javascriptCopy code

```
console.log("Hello, Node.js!");
```

You can run it in your terminal with the command:

Copy code

```
node hello.js
```

This will execute the JavaScript code, and you will see the output "Hello, Node.js!" in your terminal.

npm, on the other hand, is a powerful package manager that simplifies the process of managing project dependencies and distributing JavaScript libraries and modules. To get started with npm, you can create a **package.json** file in your project directory. This file defines your project's metadata and dependencies.

You can create a **package.json** file manually or by running the following command in your project directory:

csharpCopy code

```
npm init
```

This command will interactively guide you through the process of creating a **package.json** file, prompting you for information such as the project name, version, description, entry point, and more. Once the **package.json** file is created, you can start adding dependencies to your project using npm.

To install a package as a project dependency, you can use the **npm install** command followed by the package name. For example, to install the popular **lodash** library, you can run:

Copy code

```
npm install lodash
```

This will download and install the **lodash** package and add it as a dependency in your **package.json** file.

To use a package in your JavaScript code, you can require it using the **require** function. For example, to use **lodash** in your code, you can do the following:

javascriptCopy code

```
const _ = require('lodash');
```

You can now use functions from the **lodash** library in your code.

Additionally, npm provides a way to manage development dependencies separately from production dependencies. Development dependencies are typically tools or libraries used during the development process, such as testing frameworks or build tools. You can add a development dependency by using the **--save-dev** flag when installing a package. For example:

cssCopy code

```
npm install jest --save-dev
```

This will add **jest** as a development dependency in your **package.json** file.

Once you have added dependencies to your project, you can share your project with others by sharing the

package.json file. When someone else wants to work on your project, they can simply run **npm install** in the project directory, and npm will automatically install all the project's dependencies listed in the **package.json** file.

npm also allows you to specify version ranges for your dependencies, ensuring that your project uses compatible versions of packages. You can specify version ranges in the **dependencies** and **devDependencies** sections of your **package.json** file.

For example, you can specify a specific version of a package:

jsonCopy code

```
"dependencies": { "lodash": "4.17.21" }
```

Or you can use version ranges to allow updates within certain constraints:

jsonCopy code

```
"dependencies": { "lodash": "^4.17.21" }
```

The ^ symbol indicates that npm should install the latest minor or patch version within the same major version range.

In summary, installing Node.js and npm provides you with a powerful platform and package manager for JavaScript development. Node.js allows you to run JavaScript code on the server side, while npm simplifies the management of project dependencies and facilitates code sharing with other developers. With these tools at your disposal, you can embark on a journey of building, managing, and sharing JavaScript applications and libraries more effectively.

Configuring your Integrated Development Environment (IDE) for TypeScript development is a crucial step in harnessing the full power of TypeScript's features and capabilities. An IDE tailored for TypeScript not only enhances your coding experience but also helps you write clean and error-free code more efficiently.

The most popular IDE for TypeScript development is Visual Studio Code (VS Code), which is known for its excellent TypeScript support and a wide range of extensions that simplify the development workflow.

To configure your IDE for TypeScript development using Visual Studio Code, you'll first need to install the editor itself, which is available for Windows, macOS, and Linux.

You can download the appropriate version for your platform from the official VS Code website or use a package manager like **brew** on macOS or **chocolatey** on Windows to install it.

Once you have VS Code installed, open it, and you'll be greeted by a clean and intuitive interface. VS Code's extension system is where you can customize your development environment, and for TypeScript, the "TSLint," "Prettier," and "TypeScript Hero" extensions are popular choices.

To install extensions in VS Code, navigate to the Extensions view by clicking the square icon on the sidebar or pressing **Ctrl+Shift+X** (Windows/Linux) or **Cmd+Shift+X** (macOS).

In the Extensions view, you can search for and install extensions by typing their names into the search bar. For example, to install the "TSLint" extension, you can search for it, click the "Install" button, and VS Code will handle the installation process for you.

The "TSLint" extension helps maintain code quality by highlighting potential issues in your TypeScript code and providing suggestions for improvements.

"Prettier" is another essential extension that ensures consistent code formatting across your project. Once installed, you can configure "Prettier" to automatically format your TypeScript code whenever you save a file, which saves you from manually formatting your code and adheres to a consistent coding style.

The "TypeScript Hero" extension provides various productivity enhancements for TypeScript developers, including intelligent code completion, refactoring tools, and TypeScript-specific code navigation features.

To configure "Prettier" in VS Code, you can open the settings by clicking on the gear icon in the lower-left corner and selecting "Settings." In the settings, you can search for "Prettier" and customize its options to match your preferred code style.

Additionally, you can enable the "Format On Save" option to automatically format your TypeScript code every time you save a file. This ensures that your code remains consistently formatted and error-free throughout your project.

To configure the "TSLint" extension, you can create a **tslint.json** configuration file in your project's root directory to specify your linting rules. The rules you define in this file will govern how "TSLint" analyzes your TypeScript code and reports any issues it finds.

You can also configure specific rules and settings by accessing the settings in VS Code. By adjusting these settings, you can customize the linting behavior to match your project's requirements and coding standards.

Once you have configured your IDE with these extensions and settings, you'll benefit from enhanced code quality and productivity in your TypeScript development workflow. These extensions help you catch errors, maintain consistent code formatting, and navigate your TypeScript projects efficiently.

Another aspect of configuring your IDE for TypeScript development is leveraging its built-in support for TypeScript's static type checking. TypeScript's type system allows you to explicitly define types for variables, function parameters, and return values, which helps prevent type-related errors during development.

As you write TypeScript code in your IDE, it will provide real-time feedback and suggestions based on the defined types. This helps you catch type errors early in the development process and ensures that your code adheres to the specified types.

In addition to the built-in support for type checking, you can enhance your IDE's TypeScript capabilities further by configuring a **tsconfig.json** file for your project. This configuration file allows you to specify various TypeScript compiler options and settings.

By creating a **tsconfig.json** file in your project's root directory and customizing its settings, you can control how TypeScript compiles your code, which modules it targets, and how it handles TypeScript features and experimental features.

For example, you can specify the version of ECMAScript (ES) that TypeScript should target by setting the **target** option in your **tsconfig.json** file. This allows you to compile your TypeScript code into ES5, ES6, or another ES version based on your project's compatibility requirements.

Additionally, you can configure module resolution, source maps, and other compiler options in your **tsconfig.json** file to tailor TypeScript's behavior to your project's needs.

When you create or modify the **tsconfig.json** file, your IDE will recognize the configuration and use it to guide TypeScript's compilation process. This ensures that your code is compiled consistently and according to the specified settings.

Moreover, TypeScript's type checking and IntelliSense capabilities are greatly improved when your IDE is aware of your **tsconfig.json** file. Your IDE will use the configuration to provide better code suggestions, error checking, and code navigation features.

In summary, configuring your IDE for TypeScript development is a vital step in harnessing the full potential of TypeScript's features and enhancing your development workflow. By installing essential extensions, such as "TSLint," "Prettier," and "TypeScript Hero," you can ensure code quality, consistent formatting, and productivity improvements in your TypeScript projects.

Additionally, leveraging your IDE's built-in support for TypeScript's type checking and IntelliSense, along with customizing a **tsconfig.json** file for your project, allows you to fine-tune your TypeScript development environment to meet your project's specific requirements and coding standards.

Chapter 3: Basic Data Types in TypeScript

Understanding primitive data types is fundamental to programming and forms the building blocks of every program. These data types represent the most basic values that can be manipulated in a programming language.

In most programming languages, primitive data types fall into several categories, including numbers, strings, booleans, and special values like null and undefined.

Numbers are used to represent numerical values, both integers and floating-point numbers. They are essential for performing arithmetic operations in programming, such as addition, subtraction, multiplication, and division.

In JavaScript, for example, numbers can be defined using the **let** or **const** keyword, followed by the variable name and the assigned value. For example:

csharpCopy code

let age = 30; const pi = 3.14159;

Strings, on the other hand, are used to represent text or sequences of characters. They are enclosed in single or double quotes in many programming languages.

In Python, you can create a string variable like this:

makefileCopy code

name = "John"

Booleans are used to represent true or false values, and they are crucial for making decisions and controlling the flow of a program. They often result from logical comparisons and operations.

In Java, you can define a boolean variable like this:

arduinoCopy code

```
boolean isRaining = true;
```

Additionally, some programming languages have special values like null and undefined. Null represents the intentional absence of any object value, while undefined typically represents the absence of a declared variable or an uninitialized variable.

In JavaScript, you might encounter undefined when attempting to access a variable that hasn't been assigned a value:

javascriptCopy code

```
let x; console.log(x); // Output: undefined
```

Understanding how to work with these primitive data types is essential for effectively manipulating and managing data in your programs.

In addition to these common primitive data types, many programming languages offer variations or additional data types to handle specific use cases. For example, some languages provide data types for handling dates, times, and complex numbers.

Date and time data types are important for working with time-related information, such as scheduling events or calculating durations.

In Python, the **datetime** module offers various data types for working with dates and times:

```
javaCopy code
from datetime import datetime current_time =
datetime.now()
```

Complex numbers are used in mathematical calculations involving real and imaginary parts. They are often required in fields like engineering and physics.

Python provides a **complex** data type for working with complex numbers:

```
makefileCopy code
z = 3 + 4j
```

It's worth noting that not all programming languages have built-in support for complex numbers, so you may need to use external libraries or implement your own custom data types for such cases.

When working with primitive data types, it's essential to consider their limitations and potential issues. For example, numbers in most programming languages have finite precision, which can lead to rounding errors when performing complex calculations.

In JavaScript, you may encounter issues like this:

```
arduinoCopy code
console.log(0.1 + 0.2); // Output:
0.30000000000000004
```

To mitigate such problems, developers often rely on techniques like rounding and formatting to ensure the accuracy of numeric results.

Additionally, string manipulation can become challenging when dealing with special characters, character encoding, and escaping sequences. Proper handling of strings is crucial to avoid security vulnerabilities like injection attacks.

Booleans should be used with care to ensure that they accurately represent the intended logical conditions in your code. Misusing or misinterpreting boolean values can lead to unexpected behavior.

Understanding the behavior and characteristics of primitive data types is essential for writing efficient and reliable code. It enables you to make informed decisions when selecting the appropriate data type for your variables and ensures that your programs handle data accurately and securely.

Furthermore, many programming languages provide type conversion mechanisms that allow you to convert values from one data type to another. These conversions can be implicit or explicit, depending on the language's rules and conventions.

Implicit type conversion, also known as type coercion, occurs automatically when a value of one data type is used in a context that expects a different data type. This can lead to unexpected behavior if not understood and managed properly.

In JavaScript, for instance, type coercion can lead to surprising results when using the + operator:

arduinoCopy code

```
console.log(5 + "5"); // Output: "55"
```

To avoid such situations, it's essential to understand the rules of type coercion in your chosen programming language and explicitly convert values when necessary.

Explicit type conversion, often referred to as type casting or type conversion functions, allows you to convert values from one data type to another explicitly. This provides more control and predictability in your code.

In Python, you can use the **int()** and **str()** functions to explicitly convert between integers and strings:

makefileCopy code

```
x = "5" y = int(x) # Explicitly convert the string to an integer
```

Understanding when and how to perform explicit type conversions is vital for ensuring that your program behaves as intended and avoids unexpected errors.

Moreover, some programming languages offer mechanisms for checking the type of a value at runtime, allowing you to make decisions or perform operations based on the data type of a variable.

In Python, the **isinstance()** function is commonly used to check the type of an object:

pythonCopy code

```
x = 5 if isinstance(x, int): print("x is an integer")
```

This type-checking capability is valuable for handling different data types gracefully and preventing type-related errors in your code.

In summary, understanding primitive data types and their behavior in programming languages is fundamental for every developer. These data types form the foundation of data manipulation, calculations, and decision-making in software development.

By mastering the use of numbers, strings, booleans, and special values like null and undefined, as well as understanding more specialized data types for dates, times, and complex numbers, you can write code that is not only efficient but also accurate and reliable.

Additionally, being aware of type conversion mechanisms, both implicit and explicit, and understanding how to check the type of values at runtime provides you with the tools to handle diverse data types effectively and make informed decisions in your programming journey.

Type inference is a fundamental concept in TypeScript that allows the type of a variable to be automatically determined by the compiler based on its value. This powerful feature simplifies the development process by reducing the need for explicit type annotations while still providing strong type checking.

When you declare a variable in TypeScript without specifying its type, the TypeScript compiler uses type inference to analyze the variable's initialization and assigns an appropriate type based on the assigned value. This process occurs during the compilation phase, ensuring that type errors are caught early in the development cycle.

For example, consider the following TypeScript code snippet:

typescriptCopy code

```
let message = "Hello, TypeScript!";
```
In this example, the variable **message** is assigned a string value, so TypeScript infers its type as **string**. You didn't need to explicitly declare the type of **message**, as TypeScript automatically inferred it.

Type inference becomes particularly powerful when working with complex data structures, such as objects and arrays. TypeScript can infer the types of properties in objects and elements in arrays based on their initial values.

Let's look at an example involving an object:

typescriptCopy code
```
const person = { name: "John", age: 30, };
```
In this case, TypeScript infers the type of **person** as an object with two properties: **name**, which is of type **string**, and **age**, which is of type **number**. The type inference process examines the object's structure and assigns appropriate types to its properties.

Arrays work similarly:

typescriptCopy code
```
const numbers = [1, 2, 3, 4, 5];
```
Here, TypeScript infers the type of **numbers** as an array of numbers (**number[]**) because all the initial values are numbers.

Type inference also applies to function return types. TypeScript can determine the return type of a function based on the values it returns.

Consider the following function:

typescriptCopy code

```typescript
function add(a: number, b: number) { return a + b; }
```
In this case, TypeScript infers the return type of the **add** function as **number** because it returns the result of adding two numbers.

Type inference extends to function parameters as well. If you define a function without explicitly specifying the types of its parameters, TypeScript infers the parameter types based on the function's implementation and how it is called.

For instance:

typescriptCopy code
```typescript
function greet(name) { return "Hello, " + name + "!"; }
```

In this example, TypeScript infers the type of the **name** parameter as **any** because it couldn't determine a specific type based on the function's implementation. However, you can add type annotations to improve type safety and provide better documentation:

typescriptCopy code
```typescript
function greet(name: string) { return "Hello, " + name + "!"; }
```

Incorporating type annotations enhances code readability and helps the TypeScript compiler catch type-related errors during development.

Type inference isn't limited to simple values and functions; it also plays a crucial role in complex TypeScript features like generics and conditional types.

Generics allow you to create reusable functions, classes, or interfaces that work with various data types while maintaining type safety. Type inference helps determine the appropriate generic type based on how you use the generic construct.

Consider a simple generic function that echoes back the provided argument:

typescriptCopy code

```typescript
function echo<T>(value: T): T { return value; }
```

When you call this function, TypeScript infers the type of the return value based on the argument you provide:

typescriptCopy code

```typescript
const text = echo("Hello, TypeScript!"); // Inferred type: string const number = echo(42); // Inferred type: number
```

Type inference ensures that the returned value has the same type as the provided argument, making the function flexible and type-safe.

Conditional types, introduced in TypeScript 2.8, use type inference to create complex type conditions based on the types of other values. These types are often used in advanced scenarios to create type transformations and mappings.

For instance, you can define a conditional type that checks whether a given type is an object and, if so, extracts its keys:

typescriptCopy code

```typescript
type ObjectKeys<T> = T extends object ? keyof T : never;
```

In this example, the **ObjectKeys** type uses conditional type inference to check if the provided type **T** is an object (**T extends object**). If **T** is an object, it extracts its keys using the **keyof** operator; otherwise, it returns **never**.

Type inference for conditional types allows you to create intricate type logic that adapts to different input types dynamically.

While type inference in TypeScript is a powerful tool for improving code quality and reducing the need for explicit type annotations, there are situations where you may want to provide type annotations explicitly.

Explicit type annotations can enhance code clarity and readability, especially when dealing with complex data structures or functions with multiple parameters and return types. Additionally, type annotations can serve as documentation for the code, making it easier for other developers to understand its intended usage.

To provide explicit type annotations, you can specify the type of a variable or parameter by using a colon (**:**) followed by the desired type.

For example:

typescriptCopy code

```typescript
let age: number = 30;
```

In this case, **age** is explicitly annotated as a **number** type.

Explicit type annotations are also beneficial when working with third-party libraries or APIs that may not provide sufficient type information for the TypeScript compiler to infer.

For instance, if you're using a library that lacks type definitions, you can manually define types or use type assertions to ensure type safety.

Type assertions allow you to tell the TypeScript compiler to treat a value as a specific type, even if it can't determine that type through normal type inference.

Here's an example of a type assertion:

typescriptCopy code

```
const inputValue: unknown = "42"; const parsedValue: number = parseInt(inputValue as string);
```

In this code, we use a type assertion (**as string**) to indicate that we are confident **inputValue** is a string. This allows us to safely parse it as a number.

It's essential to use type assertions judiciously and only when you have a strong understanding of the data's actual type. Incorrect type assertions can lead to runtime errors or type-related bugs.

In summary, type inference is a powerful feature in TypeScript that automatically determines variable and function parameter types based on their values and usage. It enhances code readability, reduces the need for explicit type annotations, and provides strong type checking.

Type inference applies to primitive data types, objects, arrays, functions, generics, and conditional types, making TypeScript a versatile and flexible language for writing type-safe code.

While type inference is a valuable tool, there are cases where explicit type annotations or type assertions are necessary to provide clarity, ensure type safety, and document the code effectively. Striking the right balance between type inference and explicit type annotations is essential for writing clean, maintainable TypeScript code.

Chapter 4: Working with Variables and Constants

Declaring variables is a fundamental concept in programming, and TypeScript provides several ways to declare variables while adding type annotations to ensure type safety.

The **let** keyword is commonly used to declare variables in TypeScript when their values may change over time. For example:

typescriptCopy code

```
let age: number = 30;
```

In this declaration, **age** is declared as a variable with the type annotation **: number**, indicating that it can hold only numeric values.

Another keyword, **const**, is used to declare constants in TypeScript, where the value is immutable after assignment:

typescriptCopy code

```
const pi: number = 3.14159;
```

Here, **pi** is declared as a constant with the type annotation **: number**, ensuring that it always holds a numeric value and cannot be changed later in the code.

TypeScript also provides the **var** keyword for variable declaration, but it has fallen out of favor in modern TypeScript development due to its less predictable behavior in terms of scope.

Type annotations in variable declarations are optional in TypeScript. The type inference system can often determine the variable's type based on the assigned value.

For example:

bashCopy code

```
let name = "John";
```

In this case, TypeScript infers the type of **name** as **string** because it is initialized with a string value.

When declaring variables with complex data types, such as objects or arrays, type annotations can be more informative and prevent potential issues.

For instance:

cssCopy code

```
let person: { name: string; age: number } = { name: "Alice", age: 25 };
```

Here, **person** is declared with a type annotation that explicitly specifies the structure of the object, including the **name** property of type **string** and the **age** property of type **number**.

TypeScript also allows you to declare variables using custom types or interfaces, promoting code reuse and maintainability.

Consider this example using a custom type:

yamlCopy code

```
type Point = { x: number; y: number }; let coordinates: Point = { x: 10, y: 20 };
```

In this case, **Point** is a custom type that defines the structure of a point with **x** and **y** properties, and **coordinates** is declared to be of that type.

Using interfaces provides a similar benefit:

cssCopy code

```
interface Person { name: string; age: number; } let
user: Person = { name: "Bob", age: 35 };
```

Here, the **Person** interface specifies the structure of a person object, and **user** is declared to be of that interface type.

Variables declared in TypeScript can also be assigned the **null** or **undefined** values, but the type system encourages you to use type unions to handle such scenarios.

For example:

typescriptCopy code

```
let nullableNumber: number | null = null; let
optionalString: string | undefined = undefined;
```

By using type unions (**number | null** and **string | undefined**), you explicitly indicate that the variables can hold both the primary type and **null** or **undefined**.

In cases where you're unsure about the initial value of a variable, TypeScript offers a **never** type, which signifies that the variable will never have a valid value.

For example:

typescriptCopy code

```
let neverVariable: never;
```

The **never** type is often used with functions that never return, throw exceptions, or encounter infinite loops.

When declaring variables in TypeScript, it's important to follow best practices for naming conventions. Descriptive and meaningful variable names can improve code readability and maintainability.

Consider these examples:

typescriptCopy code

```
let num1: number = 42; // Less descriptive let ageInYears: number = 30; // More descriptive
```

Using meaningful variable names, such as **ageInYears** instead of **num1**, makes the code self-documenting and easier for other developers to understand.

TypeScript also allows you to use destructuring when declaring variables. This feature simplifies the process of extracting values from objects or arrays.

For instance, to extract values from an object:

bashCopy code

```
let { firstName, lastName } = { firstName: "Alice", lastName: "Smith" };
```

Here, the variables **firstName** and **lastName** are declared and assigned the corresponding values from the object.

Similarly, destructuring can be used with arrays:

cssCopy code

```
let [first, second] = [10, 20];
```

In this example, **first** and **second** are declared and assigned values from the array.

Destructuring can also be used with custom types and interfaces:

typescriptCopy code

type Person = { name: string; age: number }; let { name, age } = { name: "Eve", age: 28 };

By using destructuring, you can extract and declare variables more succinctly and intuitively.

TypeScript also supports declaring variables without initializing them immediately. This is useful when you plan to assign a value to the variable later in your code.

For instance:

typescriptCopy code

let x: number; x = 42; // Assigning a value later

In this example, **x** is declared as a variable of type **number**, and its value is assigned at a later point in the code. TypeScript provides various variable declaration options and encourages type annotations for improved type safety and code clarity. Whether you're declaring variables with **let**, **const**, or **var**, or using custom types and interfaces, understanding the best practices and conventions for variable declarations is essential for writing clean and maintainable TypeScript code. By using meaningful variable names, providing type annotations when necessary, and following consistent coding conventions, you can make your TypeScript code more readable and robust.

Chapter 5: Conditional Statements and Loops

Conditional logic is a fundamental concept in programming, allowing you to make decisions in your code based on certain conditions. In TypeScript, one of the most commonly used tools for implementing conditional logic is the **if** statement.

The **if** statement in TypeScript allows you to execute a block of code if a specified condition evaluates to **true**. If the condition is **false**, the code block is skipped, and the program continues to the next statement.

Here's a basic example of an **if** statement in TypeScript:

typescriptCopy code

```
let temperature: number = 25; if (temperature > 30) { console.log("It's a hot day!"); }
```

In this example, the code checks whether the **temperature** variable is greater than 30. If the condition is true, it prints "It's a hot day!" to the console. Otherwise, it does nothing.

You can also use the **else** clause to specify a block of code to be executed when the condition is **false**:

typescriptCopy code

```
let temperature: number = 25; if (temperature > 30) { console.log("It's a hot day!"); } else { console.log("It's not too hot today."); }
```

In this modified example, if the temperature is not greater than 30, it will print "It's not too hot today." Additionally, TypeScript allows you to chain multiple **if** and **else if** statements together to handle multiple conditions. This is known as an "if-else if-else" ladder: typescriptCopy code

```
let temperature: number = 25; if (temperature > 30) { console.log("It's a hot day!"); } else if (temperature <= 30 && temperature >= 20) { console.log("The weather is pleasant."); } else { console.log("It's cold outside."); }
```

In this example, the code first checks if the temperature is greater than 30. If that condition is not met, it proceeds to the next **else if** condition. If none of the conditions are true, the code in the **else** block is executed.

The **if** statement in TypeScript can evaluate various types of conditions, including comparisons, logical expressions, and even the truthiness or falsiness of values. Here's an example involving a logical expression: typescriptCopy code

```
let isSunny: boolean = true; let temperature: number = 25; if (isSunny && temperature > 30) { console.log("It's a hot and sunny day!"); } else { console.log("It's not too hot or not sunny."); }
```

In this case, the code checks if both **isSunny** is **true** and **temperature** is greater than 30 to print "It's a hot and sunny day!"

TypeScript also supports the **switch** statement, which provides an alternative way to implement conditional logic. The **switch** statement allows you to compare a single value against multiple possible case values and execute code blocks based on the matching case:

cCopy code

```
let dayOfWeek: string = "Tuesday"; switch (dayOfWeek) { case "Monday": console.log("It's the start of the week."); break; case "Tuesday": console.log("It's Tuesday."); break; default: console.log("It's not Monday or Tuesday."); }
```

In this example, the code evaluates the value of **dayOfWeek** and executes the corresponding code block within the matching case. The **break** statement is used to exit the **switch** statement once a match is found.

The **if** statement is versatile and widely used in TypeScript and other programming languages for handling conditional logic. It allows you to make decisions in your code based on various conditions, making your programs more dynamic and responsive to different scenarios.

In addition to simple conditions, you can use logical operators, comparison operators, and complex expressions within **if** statements to create intricate decision-making processes.

Moreover, you can nest **if** statements inside one another to handle more complex scenarios:

typescriptCopy code

```
let isSunny: boolean = true; let temperature:
number = 25; if (isSunny) { if (temperature > 30) {
console.log("It's a hot and sunny day!"); } else {
console.log("It's sunny but not too hot."); } } else {
console.log("It's not sunny."); }
```

Here, the code first checks if it's sunny, and if so, it further evaluates the temperature to provide more specific information.

Conditional logic is a fundamental building block for writing dynamic and responsive software. Whether you're creating simple if-else statements or complex decision trees using nested if statements and logical operators, understanding how to use conditional logic effectively is crucial for writing functional and adaptable code.

In summary, the **if** statement in TypeScript is a powerful tool for implementing conditional logic, allowing you to make decisions in your code based on specified conditions. You can use **if**, **else**, and **else if** clauses to create branching logic, and you can apply various operators and expressions to handle different scenarios. Additionally, TypeScript provides the **switch** statement as an alternative for comparing a single value against multiple possible cases. Mastering conditional logic is essential for building software that can respond dynamically to various inputs and conditions.

Looping is a fundamental programming concept that allows you to execute a block of code repeatedly. In TypeScript, there are several ways to implement loops, with two of the most common being the **for** and **while** loops.

The **for** loop in TypeScript is used when you need to iterate over a sequence of values, such as an array or a range of numbers. It provides precise control over the number of iterations and the loop's termination condition.

Here's a basic example of a **for** loop in TypeScript:

typescriptCopy code

```
for (let i = 0; i < 5; i++) { console.log(`Iteration ${i}`); }
```

In this example, the loop initializes a variable **i** with an initial value of **0**. It then specifies a termination condition: the loop will continue as long as **i** is less than **5**. After each iteration, the value of **i** is incremented by **1**.

The loop body, enclosed in curly braces **{}**, contains the code to be executed during each iteration. In this case, it logs the current iteration number.

You can use the **break** statement within a **for** loop to exit the loop prematurely if a specific condition is met:

typescriptCopy code

```
for (let i = 0; i < 10; i++) { if (i === 5) { break; // Exit
the loop when i equals 5 } console.log(`Iteration
${i}`); }
```

In this modified example, the loop breaks when **i** equals **5**, preventing further iterations.

Another useful control statement is **continue**, which allows you to skip the rest of the current iteration and proceed to the next one:

typescriptCopy code

```
for (let i = 0; i < 5; i++) { if (i === 2) { continue; //
Skip the rest of the current iteration when i equals 2 }
console.log(`Iteration ${i}`); }
```

Here, when **i** equals **2**, the **continue** statement causes the loop to skip printing "Iteration 2" and continue with the next iteration.

The **for** loop is versatile and can be adapted to various scenarios by adjusting the initialization, termination condition, and increment/decrement expressions.

In contrast, the **while** loop is used when you need to repeat a block of code as long as a specified condition remains **true**. Unlike the **for** loop, which has built-in control for initialization and termination, the **while** loop provides more flexibility but requires careful handling to prevent infinite loops.

Here's a basic example of a **while** loop in TypeScript:

typescriptCopy code

```typescript
let counter = 0; while (counter < 5) {
console.log(`Iteration ${counter}`); counter++; //
Increment the counter }
```

In this example, the **while** loop continues as long as the **counter** is less than **5**. The loop body prints the current iteration number, and the **counter** is incremented at the end of each iteration to avoid an infinite loop.

It's crucial to ensure that the loop's termination condition is eventually met in a **while** loop. Otherwise, the loop will run indefinitely, causing your program to become unresponsive.

Similar to the **for** loop, you can use the **break** and **continue** statements within a **while** loop to control its behavior. For example:

typescriptCopy code

```typescript
let counter = 0; while (counter < 10) { if (counter
=== 7) { break; // Exit the loop when counter equals
7 } console.log(`Iteration ${counter}`); counter++; //
Increment the counter }
```

In this modified example, the **while** loop exits when **counter** equals **7**.

The **continue** statement can also be used within a **while** loop to skip the rest of the current iteration and proceed to the next one, similar to the **for** loop.

Both the **for** and **while** loops are essential tools for controlling the flow of your TypeScript programs. The choice between them depends on your specific requirements and coding style.

The **for** loop is often preferred when you know the exact number of iterations or when you need to iterate over a sequence of values, such as an array. It provides a compact and structured way to manage loops with clear initialization, termination conditions, and increments.

On the other hand, the **while** loop offers more flexibility and is suitable for scenarios where the termination condition may not be as straightforward or when you want to continuously repeat an action until a specific condition is met.

In addition to the **for** and **while** loops, TypeScript also supports the **do-while** loop, which guarantees that the loop body is executed at least once, as the condition is evaluated after the loop body.

Here's an example of a **do-while** loop:

typescriptCopy code

```
let counter = 0; do { console.log(`Iteration ${counter}`); counter++; } while (counter < 3);
```

In this case, the loop body is executed once before checking the termination condition. The loop continues as long as **counter** is less than **3**.

Looping is a crucial skill for writing dynamic and repetitive code in TypeScript. Whether you choose the **for**, **while**, or **do-while** loop, understanding how to control the flow of your code using loops is essential for building efficient and functional TypeScript applications.

By mastering the use of loops and combining them with conditional statements, you can create powerful and responsive programs that perform a wide range of tasks, from data processing to user interface interactions.

Chapter 6: Functions and Scope in TypeScript

Function scope and closures are fundamental concepts in JavaScript and TypeScript that govern how variables and functions are accessible within different parts of your code.

In JavaScript, each function creates its own scope, which means that variables declared inside a function are typically not accessible from outside that function. Let's start by exploring function scope:

When you declare a variable using the **var** keyword within a function, it becomes function-scoped, which means it can only be accessed within that function.

For example:

typescriptCopy code

```
function greet() { var message = "Hello, TypeScript!"; console.log(message); } greet();
console.log(message); // Throws an error: "message is not defined"
```

In this example, the variable **message** is declared inside the **greet** function and can be accessed and used within that function. However, attempting to access **message** outside the function results in an error because it is not defined in that scope.

It's important to note that variables declared with **var** are function-scoped, which can lead to unexpected behavior in some situations. For this reason, it's generally recommended to use **let** and **const** for variable declarations in modern JavaScript and TypeScript code.

Variables declared with **let** and **const** have block scope, which means they are limited to the block or statement where they are defined. A block can be a function, a loop, an if statement, or any set of curly braces {}.

Here's an example using **let**:

typescriptCopy code

```
function greet() { let message = "Hello, TypeScript!";
console.log(message);             }              greet();
console.log(message); // Throws an error: "message
is not defined"
```

In this updated code, **let** is used to declare **message**, and it behaves similarly to **var** within the function scope.

However, when it comes to block scope, **let** and **const** shine. They allow you to declare variables within blocks and limit their visibility to those blocks:

typescriptCopy code

```
if (true) { let blockScoped = "I am in a block";
console.log(blockScoped); // "I am in a block" }
console.log(blockScoped); // Throws an error:
"blockScoped is not defined"
```

In this example, **blockScoped** is declared within the **if** block and is only accessible within that block. Attempting to access it outside the block results in an error.

Now, let's delve into closures:

Closures are a powerful and somewhat advanced concept in JavaScript and TypeScript. They occur when a function is defined within another function and has access to the outer function's variables. Closures "close over" variables from their containing scope, allowing you to create private variables and maintain state.

Here's an example of a closure:

typescriptCopy code

```
function outer() { let message = "Hello, "; function inner(name) { console.log(message + name); } return inner; } const sayHello = outer(); sayHello("Alice"); // "Hello, Alice"
```

In this code, **outer** defines a variable **message** and an inner function **inner**. **inner** has access to **message**, even after **outer** has finished executing, because it forms a closure over **message**. When **sayHello** is called with the name "Alice," it can still access and use **message** from the scope of **outer**.

Closures are often used to encapsulate state or create private variables within functions. They allow you to maintain data within a function and expose only the necessary functionality through returned functions or objects.

Here's an example of using closures to create a counter:

typescriptCopy code

```
function counter() { let count = 0; return {
increment: function () { count++; }, decrement:
function () { count--; }, getValue: function () { return
count; }, }; } const myCounter = counter();
myCounter.increment(); myCounter.increment();
console.log(myCounter.getValue()); // 2
```

In this example, the **counter** function creates a closure around the **count** variable. The returned object exposes methods to increment, decrement, and retrieve the current value of the counter while keeping the **count** variable private.

Closures can be powerful tools for managing state, implementing data hiding, and creating reusable and modular code.

However, it's essential to understand that closures can also lead to memory leaks if not used carefully. When a function forms a closure over variables, those variables continue to exist in memory as long as the closure is referenced. Therefore, excessive closures can lead to increased memory consumption, especially if they capture large data structures.

In summary, understanding function scope and closures is crucial for writing effective JavaScript and TypeScript code. Function scope determines the visibility of variables within functions, and using **let** and **const** with block scope is recommended for modern code.

Closures, on the other hand, allow inner functions to access variables from their containing scope, enabling powerful patterns like data encapsulation and private variables. Closures are a key concept for creating modular and maintainable code, but they should be used judiciously to avoid memory-related issues.

By mastering these concepts, you'll be better equipped to write clean, efficient, and well-structured code in TypeScript and JavaScript.

Chapter 7: Arrays and Objects

Arrays are fundamental data structures in TypeScript, and they play a vital role in many programming tasks. One of the most common operations when working with arrays is adding elements to it. To add elements to the end of an array, you can use the **push** method. For example:

typescriptCopy code

```
let fruits: string[] = ["apple", "banana", "cherry"];
fruits.push("date");
```

In this code, the **push** method adds the string "date" to the end of the **fruits** array.

You can also add elements to the beginning of an array using the **unshift** method:

typescriptCopy code

```
let fruits: string[] = ["apple", "banana", "cherry"];
fruits.unshift("date");
```

Now, the array **fruits** contains "date" as its first element.

To remove elements from the end of an array, you can use the **pop** method:

typescriptCopy code

```
let fruits: string[] = ["apple", "banana", "cherry"];
let removedFruit = fruits.pop();
```

After executing this code, **removedFruit** will contain the string "cherry," and the **fruits** array will no longer have "cherry" as its last element.

Similarly, you can remove elements from the beginning of an array using the **shift** method:

typescriptCopy code

```typescript
let fruits: string[] = ["apple", "banana", "cherry"];
let removedFruit = fruits.shift();
```

In this case, **removedFruit** will contain the string "apple," and the **fruits** array will no longer have "apple" as its first element.

To insert elements at a specific position in an array, you can use the **splice** method. The **splice** method allows you to specify the index where you want to start adding or removing elements and the number of elements to remove (if any).

Here's an example of adding elements at a specific position:

typescriptCopy code

```typescript
let fruits: string[] = ["apple", "banana", "cherry"];
fruits.splice(1, 0, "date", "fig");
```

In this code, **splice(1, 0, "date", "fig")** inserts the strings "date" and "fig" at index 1 (after "apple") without removing any elements. The **fruits** array will now be **["apple", "date", "fig", "banana", "cherry"]**.

You can also use **splice** to remove elements from a specific position:

typescriptCopy code

```typescript
let fruits: string[] = ["apple", "banana", "cherry"];
fruits.splice(1, 2);
```

In this example, **splice(1, 2)** removes two elements starting from index 1. After executing this code, the **fruits** array will be **["apple"]**.

Another common array manipulation technique is creating a copy of an array. TypeScript provides several ways to create a shallow copy of an array.

One simple method is using the spread operator (**...**):

typescriptCopy code

```
let originalArray: number[] = [1, 2, 3]; let copiedArray: number[] = [...originalArray];
```

Here, **copiedArray** is a shallow copy of **originalArray**.

You can also use the **slice** method to create a copy of a portion of an array:

typescriptCopy code

```
let originalArray: number[] = [1, 2, 3, 4, 5]; let copiedArray: number[] = originalArray.slice(2, 4);
```

In this example, **copiedArray** will contain **[3, 4]**, which is a copy of the elements at index 2 and 3 of **originalArray**.

When dealing with arrays of objects, it's important to note that these methods create shallow copies. This means that if the original array contains objects, the copied array will still reference the same objects, not their copies.

To create a deep copy of an array containing objects, you may need to use custom methods or libraries specifically designed for deep copying.

Sorting arrays is a common operation when working with data. TypeScript provides the **sort** method to sort the elements of an array in place.

Here's an example of sorting an array of numbers in ascending order:

typescriptCopy code

```
let numbers: number[] = [3, 1, 4, 1, 5, 9, 2, 6, 5, 3, 5]; numbers.sort((a, b) => a - b);
```

After executing this code, the **numbers** array will be sorted in ascending order: **[1, 1, 2, 3, 3, 4, 5, 5, 5, 6, 9]**.

You can also sort an array of strings alphabetically:

typescriptCopy code

```
let fruits: string[] = ["apple", "banana", "cherry", "date", "fig"]; fruits.sort();
```

In this case, the **fruits** array will be sorted alphabetically: **["apple", "banana", "cherry", "date", "fig"]**.

The **sort** method also allows you to provide a custom sorting function to handle more complex sorting criteria.

Reversing the order of elements in an array can be accomplished using the **reverse** method:

typescriptCopy code

```
let fruits: string[] = ["apple", "banana", "cherry"]; fruits.reverse();
```

After executing this code, the **fruits** array will be reversed: **["cherry", "banana", "apple"]**.

Mapping is another common operation when working with arrays. The **map** method allows you to transform each element of an array and create a new array with the transformed values.

For example, you can convert an array of numbers to an array of their squares:

typescriptCopy code

```
let numbers: number[] = [1, 2, 3, 4, 5]; let squares: number[] = numbers.map((number) => number * number);
```

After executing this code, the **squares** array will contain **[1, 4, 9, 16, 25]**.

The **map** method applies the provided function to each element of the array and creates a new array with the results.

Another common operation is filtering an array to create a new array containing only the elements that meet specific criteria. TypeScript provides the **filter** method for this purpose.

Here's an example of filtering even numbers from an array of numbers:

typescriptCopy code

```
let numbers: number[] = [1, 2, 3, 4, 5]; let evenNumbers: number[] = numbers.filter((number) => number % 2 === 0);
```

After executing this code, the **evenNumbers** array will contain **[2, 4]**.

The **filter** method evaluates the provided function for each element in the array and includes only the elements for which the function returns **true** in the new array.

Additionally, TypeScript offers the **reduce** method, which allows you to accumulate values from an array into a single result. This is useful for performing operations like summing up the elements of an array.

Here's an example of using **reduce** to calculate the sum of an array of numbers:

typescriptCopy code

```
let numbers: number[] = [1, 2, 3, 4, 5]; let sum: number = numbers.reduce((accumulator, currentValue) => accumulator + currentValue, 0);
```

In this code, **reduce** starts with an initial value of **0** for the **accumulator** and iterates through the **numbers** array, adding each element to the accumulator.

After executing this code, the **sum** variable will contain the value **15**, which is the sum of all the elements in the **numbers** array.

Arrays in TypeScript are versatile and offer a wide range of methods for manipulating their contents. Whether you need to add or remove elements, create copies, sort, map, filter, or reduce, TypeScript provides the tools and techniques to efficiently work with arrays in your programs.

By mastering these array manipulation techniques, you can write more efficient and expressive code for various tasks, from data processing to creating dynamic user interfaces.

Objects and interfaces are fundamental concepts in TypeScript, allowing you to define and work with structured data.

In TypeScript, an object is a collection of key-value pairs where each key is a string (or symbol) and each value can be of any data type, including other objects. Creating an object in TypeScript is straightforward:

typescriptCopy code

```
let person = { firstName: "John", lastName: "Doe", age: 30, };
```

In this example, we define an object **person** with three properties: **firstName**, **lastName**, and **age**, each associated with a value.

You can access the properties of an object using dot notation:

typescriptCopy code

```
console.log(person.firstName);        //       "John"
console.log(person.age); // 30
```

Alternatively, you can use bracket notation to access object properties by their names as strings:

typescriptCopy code

```
console.log(person["firstName"]);        //       "John"
console.log(person["age"]); // 30
```

Objects in TypeScript are dynamic, meaning you can add or modify properties after the object is created:

typescriptCopy code

```
person.city = "New York"; person.age = 31;
```

Now, the **person** object has two additional properties: **city** and an updated **age**.

You can also use the **delete** operator to remove properties from an object:

typescriptCopy code

```
delete person.age;
```

After executing this code, the **person** object no longer has the **age** property.

Objects can contain complex data structures, including arrays and other objects. Here's an example of an object with nested objects and arrays:

typescriptCopy code

```
let student = { name: "Alice", grades: [95, 89, 97],
address: { street: "123 Main St", city: "Anytown", },
};
```

In this case, the **student** object has a **grades** property that is an array of numbers and an **address** property that is another object with **street** and **city** properties.

Working with interfaces is a crucial aspect of TypeScript, as they define the structure and shape of objects in your code. Interfaces allow you to enforce type checking and provide documentation for your objects.

To define an interface in TypeScript, you use the **interface** keyword followed by the interface's name and the structure of the object it describes. Here's an example:

typescriptCopy code

```typescript
interface Person { firstName: string; lastName: string; age: number; }
```

In this code, we've defined an interface **Person** that specifies the structure of a person object, including the **firstName**, **lastName**, and **age** properties.

You can use an interface to create objects that adhere to its structure:

typescriptCopy code

```typescript
let person: Person = { firstName: "John", lastName: "Doe", age: 30, };
```

In this example, the **person** object conforms to the **Person** interface.

Interfaces are not limited to simple properties; they can also describe functions within objects. For instance, you can define an interface for an object representing a mathematical operation:

typescriptCopy code

```typescript
interface Operation { name: string; perform: (x: number, y: number) => number; }
```

Here, the **Operation** interface includes a **name** property and a **perform** function that takes two numbers as arguments and returns a number.

You can then implement this interface to create objects that perform specific operations:

typescriptCopy code

```typescript
let addition: Operation = { name: "Addition", perform: (x, y) => x + y, }; let multiplication:
```

Operation = { name: "Multiplication", perform: (x, y) => x * y, };

Both **addition** and **multiplication** objects conform to the **Operation** interface, providing the required properties and methods.

Interfaces also support optional properties, allowing you to specify that certain properties may or may not exist in objects that implement the interface:

typescriptCopy code

interface Person { firstName: string; lastName: string; age?: number; }

In this modified **Person** interface, the **age** property is marked as optional by adding a **?** after its name. This means objects implementing the interface can have an **age** property or omit it altogether.

Interfaces can also define readonly properties, which are properties that can't be modified once an object is created:

typescriptCopy code

interface Point { readonly x: number; readonly y: number; }

In this example, the **Point** interface defines **x** and **y** as readonly properties, meaning you can't change their values after creating an object that implements the interface.

Working with objects and interfaces in TypeScript enables you to create structured, type-safe code. Interfaces define the structure and shape of objects, helping you catch type errors at compile time and providing clear documentation for your code.

It's important to note that TypeScript's type inference often allows you to work with objects without explicitly defining interfaces. However, using interfaces enhances code readability, maintainability, and collaboration in larger codebases.

In addition to creating objects and interfaces, TypeScript provides a range of advanced techniques for working with objects, including inheritance, type assertions, and destructuring objects.

Inheritance allows you to create new interfaces by extending existing ones, inheriting their properties and methods. This promotes code reuse and maintains consistency across related interfaces.

Type assertions are used to inform TypeScript that you know more about the type of an object than TypeScript does, allowing you to access properties or call methods that TypeScript wouldn't normally allow.

Destructuring objects is a convenient way to extract properties from objects and assign them to variables, simplifying the process of working with complex objects. Overall, mastering objects and interfaces in TypeScript is essential for writing robust and maintainable code, particularly in larger projects or when collaborating with other developers. By leveraging these features, you can create structured and type-safe code that is easier to understand, maintain, and extend.

Chapter 8: Introduction to TypeScript Classes

Constructors and class inheritance are fundamental concepts in object-oriented programming (OOP) and are crucial for creating reusable and organized code in TypeScript.

In OOP, a constructor is a special method that is automatically called when an object is created from a class.

In TypeScript, you can define a constructor method using the **constructor** keyword within a class. This constructor method can initialize the object's properties or perform other setup tasks.

Here's an example of a simple class with a constructor:

typescriptCopy code

```
class Person { firstName: string; lastName: string;
constructor(firstName: string, lastName: string) {
this.firstName = firstName; this.lastName =
lastName; } }
```

In this code, we have defined a **Person** class with two properties, **firstName** and **lastName**. The constructor method takes two parameters, **firstName** and **lastName**, and assigns their values to the corresponding properties.

When you create an instance of the **Person** class, the constructor is automatically called, and you can pass values for the **firstName** and **lastName** properties to initialize the object:

typescriptCopy code

let johnDoe = new Person("John", "Doe");

Now, **johnDoe** is an instance of the **Person** class with the **firstName** and **lastName** properties set to "John" and "Doe," respectively.

Constructors can be used to perform various initialization tasks, such as setting default values, connecting to databases, or performing other setup operations specific to the class.

Inheritance is a key concept in OOP that allows you to create a new class (a subclass or derived class) that inherits properties and methods from an existing class (a superclass or base class). This promotes code reuse and hierarchy in your application's object structure.

In TypeScript, you can achieve inheritance by using the **extends** keyword when defining a subclass. The subclass inherits all the properties and methods of the superclass and can also have its own additional properties and methods.

Here's an example of class inheritance in TypeScript:

typescriptCopy code

```
class Animal { name: string; constructor(name:
string) { this.name = name; } makeSound() {
console.log("Some generic animal sound"); } } class
Dog extends Animal { breed: string;
constructor(name: string, breed: string) {
super(name); // Call the constructor of the superclass
```

```
this.breed = breed; } makeSound() {
console.log("Woof! Woof!"); } }
```

In this code, we have defined two classes: **Animal** and **Dog**. The **Dog** class extends the **Animal** class using the **extends** keyword.

The **Animal** class has a **name** property and a **makeSound** method, while the **Dog** class adds a **breed** property and overrides the **makeSound** method with its own implementation.

To create an instance of the **Dog** class, you can use its constructor, which also calls the constructor of the superclass (**Animal**) using the **super** keyword:

typescriptCopy code

```
let myDog = new Dog("Buddy", "Golden Retriever");
```

Now, **myDog** is an instance of the **Dog** class with the **name** property inherited from the **Animal** class and the **breed** property specific to the **Dog** class.

Inheritance allows you to create a hierarchy of classes, where each class can specialize and extend the behavior of its superclass. This enables you to model complex relationships and structures in your application.

In TypeScript, you can also use the **super** keyword to access methods or properties of the superclass within the subclass. This is useful when you want to reuse or extend the functionality of the superclass.

For example, you can call the **makeSound** method of the superclass within the **Dog** class using **super**:

typescriptCopy code

```
class Dog extends Animal { // ... makeSound() {
super.makeSound();  // Call the superclass's
makeSound method console.log("Woof! Woof!"); } }
```

In this modified **Dog** class, the **makeSound** method first calls the **makeSound** method of the superclass (**Animal**) using **super.makeSound()**. It then adds its own implementation.

By using the **super** keyword, you can build upon the behavior of the superclass while customizing and extending it in the subclass.

Another important concept in class inheritance is method overriding. When a subclass provides its own implementation of a method that is already defined in the superclass, it is said to override that method.

In TypeScript, method overriding allows you to change or extend the behavior of a method in the subclass while keeping the same method signature (name and parameters) as in the superclass.

Here's an example of method overriding in TypeScript:

typescriptCopy code

```
class Animal { makeSound() { console.log("Some
generic animal sound"); } } class Dog extends
Animal { makeSound() { console.log("Woof!
Woof!"); } }
```

In this code, the **Dog** class overrides the **makeSound** method inherited from the **Animal** class. When you create an instance of **Dog** and call its **makeSound** method, it will execute the overridden implementation, which outputs "Woof! Woof!" instead of the generic animal sound.

Method overriding allows you to specialize and customize the behavior of a method in a subclass while maintaining a consistent interface with the superclass.

Inheritance in TypeScript supports multiple levels of hierarchy, meaning you can have classes that extend other subclasses, forming a tree-like structure. This enables you to model complex relationships and share common behavior across various parts of your application.

However, it's essential to use inheritance judiciously and consider other object-oriented principles like composition and interfaces when designing your class hierarchy. Overusing inheritance can lead to tight coupling and complex dependencies between classes.

In summary, constructors and class inheritance are fundamental concepts in TypeScript that enable you to create and organize your code in a structured and reusable manner. Constructors allow you to initialize objects, while inheritance allows you to create hierarchies of classes and promote code reuse.

By understanding and effectively using constructors and inheritance, you can design more modular and maintainable code in TypeScript, making it easier to build and extend your applications.

Chapter 9: Error Handling and Debugging

Handling errors is a crucial aspect of software development, and TypeScript provides powerful mechanisms to manage and recover from errors that may occur during the execution of your code.

One common approach to handling errors is using the **try...catch** statement, which allows you to wrap a section of code that might generate exceptions and then define how to respond when an exception occurs.

The **try** block encloses the code that you want to monitor for exceptions, while the **catch** block specifies what to do when an exception is thrown. The **catch** block contains the code that will be executed when an exception occurs in the **try** block.

Here's a basic example of using **try...catch** in TypeScript:

typescriptCopy code

```
try { // Code that may throw an exception let result
= 10 / 0; // This will throw a division by zero error }
catch (error) { // Code to handle the exception
console.error("An error occurred:", error); }
```

In this example, the **try** block contains code that attempts to perform a division by zero operation, which is invalid and will throw a runtime error. When the error occurs, the program flow is redirected to the **catch** block, where you can handle the error.

The **catch** block accepts an error parameter (in this case, named **error**) that contains information about the error, such as its message and stack trace. You can use this information to log the error, display a user-friendly message, or take appropriate corrective actions.

It's important to note that **try...catch** only captures exceptions that occur within the **try** block. If an exception is thrown in a function called from within the **try** block, it can still be caught by the closest surrounding **catch** block.

In addition to catching exceptions, TypeScript allows you to specify the type of exception that you want to catch. This can be useful when you want to handle specific types of errors differently.

For example, you can catch a specific error type, such as **Error**:

typescriptCopy code

```
try { // Code that may throw an Error throw new Error("This is a custom error"); } catch (error) { if (error instanceof Error) { console.error("An Error occurred:", error.message); } else { console.error("An unknown error occurred."); } }
```

In this code, we explicitly catch the **Error** type, which is a common base type for errors in TypeScript. We then check if the caught error is an instance of **Error** before handling it.

It's essential to choose meaningful error types to catch and handle specific exceptions effectively in your application.

In addition to the **catch** block, TypeScript also supports the optional **finally** block, which allows you to define code that will be executed regardless of whether an exception occurs or not.

Here's an example with a **finally** block:

typescriptCopy code

```
try { // Code that may throw an exception
console.log("Inside try block"); } catch (error) {
console.error("An error occurred:", error); } finally {
console.log("This code always runs"); }
```

In this code, the **finally** block contains code that will be executed whether or not an exception is thrown in the **try** block. It's useful for performing cleanup operations or releasing resources, such as closing files or database connections.

You can use **try...catch** in various scenarios, such as when dealing with external APIs, file operations, network requests, or user input validation. By handling exceptions gracefully, you can prevent your application from crashing and provide a better user experience.

Custom Error Handling: While catching built-in error types is common, you can also define custom error classes to handle specific application-specific exceptions. Custom errors can provide more context and information about the problem, making it easier to troubleshoot and debug issues in your code.

Here's an example of creating a custom error class in TypeScript:

typescriptCopy code

```
class CustomError extends Error { constructor(message: string) { super(message); this.name = "CustomError"; } }
```

In this code, we define a **CustomError** class that extends the built-in **Error** class. We set a custom name for our error class to differentiate it from other error types.

You can throw instances of your custom error class like this:

typescriptCopy code

```
try { // Code that may throw a custom error  throw new CustomError("This is a custom error"); } catch (error) { if (error instanceof CustomError) { console.error("A custom error occurred:", error.message); } else { console.error("An unknown error occurred."); } }
```

By defining and throwing custom error classes, you can add more context to your error handling and provide better information about the specific issues that arise in your application.

When working with asynchronous code, error handling becomes even more critical, as exceptions may occur at different points in time, and traditional **try...catch** blocks may not be sufficient.

In asynchronous code, you can use the **try...catch** approach in combination with **async/await** to handle errors gracefully. The **await** keyword allows you to pause the execution of asynchronous code until a promise is resolved or rejected.

Here's an example of using **try...catch** with **async/await** in TypeScript:

typescriptCopy code

```
async function fetchData() { try { const response = await fetch("https://api.example.com/data"); if (!response.ok) { throw new Error("Failed to fetch data"); } const data = await response.json(); return data; } catch (error) { console.error("An error occurred:", error.message); throw error; // Rethrow the error to propagate it to the caller } }
```

In this code, we define an **async** function **fetchData** that fetches data from an API using the **fetch** function. We use **await** to handle the asynchronous operations and check the response status.

If an error occurs during the fetch operation, we throw a custom error with a descriptive message. The **try...catch** block catches and handles the error, logging a message.

It's important to note that when you catch an error inside an **async** function, you can choose to handle it locally or rethrow it to propagate it to the caller.

Rethrowing allows higher-level code to handle the error as needed.

In summary, error handling is an essential part of writing robust and reliable TypeScript applications. The **try...catch** statement provides a structured way to handle exceptions and recover gracefully from errors.

By using **try...catch** effectively, you can prevent unexpected crashes, log meaningful error messages, and ensure a smoother user experience. Custom error classes and **async/await** support enhance your ability to handle errors in a more structured and expressive manner, allowing you to create more resilient applications.

Chapter 10: Building Your First TypeScript Project

Structuring a TypeScript project effectively is crucial for maintaining code organization, scalability, and collaboration among developers.

One commonly used project structure for TypeScript is based on the principles of modularization, separation of concerns, and clear directory organization.

At the heart of any TypeScript project is the source code, which typically resides in a dedicated directory. This directory often has a clear and descriptive name like "src" (short for "source") to indicate its purpose.

Inside the "src" directory, you organize your TypeScript code into modules and files. Modules are logical units that group related functionality together, making it easier to manage and reuse code.

For example, you might have a module for user authentication, another for data retrieval, and one for user interface components. Each module should have its own TypeScript file, and you can create subdirectories within "src" to further organize related modules.

To create a new TypeScript module, simply create a ".ts" file within the appropriate directory. TypeScript modules can export classes, functions, variables, and other constructs that can be imported and used in other parts of your project.

Here's an example of a simple TypeScript module:
typescriptCopy code

```
// src/auth.ts  class  AuthService { // Implementation
of authentication logic } export default AuthService;
```

In this code, we've defined an **AuthService** class in a module called "auth.ts." The **export default** statement makes this class available for import in other parts of the project.

One of the key benefits of TypeScript is its strong type system, which helps catch errors and provide better code documentation. To fully leverage TypeScript's type checking, it's essential to configure your project to use TypeScript's strict mode.

To enable strict mode, you can add the **"strict": true** option in your "tsconfig.json" file, which is the TypeScript configuration file for your project. Strict mode enforces stricter type checking rules and helps you write safer and more maintainable code.

Here's an example of a "tsconfig.json" file with strict mode enabled:
jsonCopy code

```
{ "compilerOptions": { "strict": true } }
```

In addition to strict mode, TypeScript offers various other configuration options to customize how your code is compiled and checked. You can specify target ECMAScript versions, module systems (CommonJS, ES6, etc.), and many other settings in your "tsconfig.json" file to match your project's requirements.

TypeScript projects often involve working with external libraries and dependencies. Managing these dependencies is essential for a smooth development experience.

To manage dependencies, TypeScript projects commonly use package managers like npm (Node Package Manager) or Yarn. These package managers allow you to install, update, and remove packages easily.

To initialize a new TypeScript project with npm, you can run the following command in your project's root directory:

csharpCopy code

```
npm init
```

This command prompts you to provide information about your project and creates a "package.json" file that lists your project's dependencies and configuration.

To install TypeScript as a development dependency, you can run:

cssCopy code

```
npm install typescript --save-dev
```

This command installs TypeScript and adds it to the "devDependencies" section of your "package.json" file.

Once TypeScript is installed, you can use npm or yarn to install other dependencies your project may need, such as web frameworks, libraries, or tools.

Managing dependencies in your TypeScript project allows you to leverage existing libraries and tools, reducing development time and effort.

When it comes to structuring a TypeScript project, you should also consider the build and deployment process. TypeScript code needs to be compiled into JavaScript before it can run in a browser or on a server.

To automate the build process, you can use a task runner or build tool like webpack, gulp, or npm scripts. These tools can help you compile TypeScript files, bundle assets, and perform other build-related tasks.

Here's an example of configuring TypeScript compilation using npm scripts in your "package.json" file:

jsonCopy code

```
{ "scripts": { "build": "tsc" } }
```

In this configuration, running the **npm run build** command will trigger the TypeScript compiler (**tsc**) to compile your TypeScript files into JavaScript.

Depending on your project's needs, you may also configure additional tasks, such as minification, transpilation, or asset optimization, in your build process.

Deployment of a TypeScript project depends on your project's type and target platform. For web applications, you typically need to host your compiled JavaScript files, HTML templates, stylesheets, and other assets on a web server.

To deploy a web application, you can use a variety of hosting options, including cloud providers like AWS, Azure, or Firebase, as well as traditional web hosting services.

For server-side TypeScript applications, you may deploy them to a cloud platform like AWS Lambda, Google Cloud Functions, or a traditional web server like Apache or Nginx.

The deployment process often involves setting up deployment scripts or pipelines to automate the deployment steps. Tools like Docker and Kubernetes can be used to containerize and orchestrate your TypeScript applications in a scalable and manageable way.

In summary, structuring a TypeScript project involves organizing your source code into modules, enabling TypeScript's strict mode, managing dependencies with package managers, and configuring a build and deployment process. By following best practices for project structure, you can create maintainable and scalable TypeScript applications that are easier to develop and deploy.

Running and testing your TypeScript application is a crucial step in the development process, ensuring that your code behaves as expected and meets the desired functionality.

Before running your TypeScript application, you need to compile it into JavaScript, as browsers and Node.js primarily understand JavaScript.

The TypeScript compiler, tsc, is responsible for this task, and it's essential to have it correctly set up in your development environment.

You can compile a TypeScript file using the following command:

Copy code

```
tsc filename.ts
```

Replace **filename.ts** with the name of your TypeScript file. Running this command will generate a corresponding JavaScript file in the same directory.

To compile all TypeScript files in your project, you can use the **--project** or **-p** flag followed by the path to your tsconfig.json file:

cssCopy code

```
tsc --project tsconfig.json
```

This command compiles all TypeScript files based on the configuration settings in your tsconfig.json file.

After compiling your TypeScript code, you can execute the resulting JavaScript using Node.js or a web browser.

For server-side TypeScript applications, Node.js is the runtime environment of choice. To run a TypeScript file with Node.js, use the following command:

Copy code

```
node filename.js
```

Replace **filename.js** with the name of the generated JavaScript file.

When developing web applications, you typically run your TypeScript code in a web browser. To do this, you need to create an HTML file that references the compiled JavaScript file in a **<script>** tag.

Here's an example of an HTML file that runs your compiled TypeScript code:

htmlCopy code

```html
<!DOCTYPE html> <html> <head> <title>My TypeScript App</title> </head> <body> <script src="app.js"></script> </body> </html>
```

In this HTML file, we include the JavaScript file generated by TypeScript using the **<script>** tag.

Once you've set up your development environment and compiled your TypeScript code, it's essential to thoroughly test your application to ensure it functions correctly.

Testing is a critical aspect of software development, as it helps identify and fix bugs, verify that new features work as expected, and maintain the overall quality of your codebase.

One of the most common approaches to testing TypeScript applications is unit testing. Unit tests focus on individual components or functions to verify their correctness in isolation.

There are several popular JavaScript testing frameworks and libraries that work seamlessly with TypeScript, such as Jest, Mocha, Chai, and Jasmine.

Jest, for instance, is a widely used testing framework that provides a simple and intuitive way to write unit tests for JavaScript and TypeScript code. To get started with Jest, you can install it as a development dependency:

cssCopy code

npm install jest --save-dev

Once installed, you can create test files with the .test.ts or .spec.ts extension to indicate that they contain tests. For example, if you have a file called math.ts with functions you want to test, you can create a math.test.ts file:

typescriptCopy code

```
// math.ts export function add(a: number, b: number): number { return a + b; }
```

typescriptCopy code

```
// math.test.ts import { add } from './math'; test('adds 1 + 2 to equal 3', () => { expect(add(1, 2)).toBe(3); });
```

In this example, we've written a simple unit test using Jest. We import the add function from our math module and use the **test** function provided by Jest to define a test case.

The **expect** function is used to make assertions, checking if the result of **add(1, 2)** equals 3. If the assertion fails, Jest will report the error and provide detailed information about the failure.

To run your Jest tests, you can add a test script to your package.json file:

jsonCopy code

```
{ "scripts": { "test": "jest" } }
```

Then, you can execute your tests with the following command:

bashCopy code

npm test

This will run all test files in your project and provide feedback on the test results.

In addition to unit testing, integration testing and end-to-end testing are essential for more complex applications.

Integration tests verify that different components or modules work together as expected, testing the interaction between them.

End-to-end tests, on the other hand, simulate the entire user journey through an application, from start to finish, to ensure that the application behaves correctly from a user's perspective.

Cypress and Puppeteer are popular tools for end-to-end testing TypeScript applications, providing a way to automate interactions with web applications and verify their functionality.

To set up Cypress for end-to-end testing, you can install it as a development dependency:

cssCopy code

npm install cypress --save-dev

After installation, you can initialize Cypress in your project with the following command:

arduinoCopy code

npx cypress open

Cypress will create a directory structure for your tests and open a graphical interface for test management.

You can write end-to-end tests in TypeScript by creating .ts files within the Cypress "integration" folder.

Here's an example of an end-to-end test using Cypress in TypeScript:

typescriptCopy code

```
// cypress/integration/example.spec.ts describe('My App', () => { it('successfully loads', () => { cy.visit('/'); }); it('contains a welcome message', () => { cy.contains('Welcome to My App'); }); });
```

In this test, we use Cypress commands like **cy.visit** and **cy.contains** to interact with the application and make assertions about its behavior.

Running your Cypress tests is as simple as running the Cypress test runner:

arduinoCopy code

```
npx cypress run
```

Cypress will execute your tests in a headless browser and provide a detailed report of the test results.

In addition to unit testing and end-to-end testing, TypeScript projects can benefit from other testing techniques, such as snapshot testing, property-based testing, and performance testing, depending on your specific requirements.

Snapshot testing, provided by libraries like Jest and React Testing Library, allows you to capture and compare snapshots of rendered components to detect unexpected changes.

Property-based testing libraries like fast-check and jsverify enable you to generate and test a large number of input values to ensure the correctness of your code under various conditions.

Performance testing tools like Apache JMeter and Google Lighthouse help you assess the performance and responsiveness of your web applications.

In summary, running and testing your TypeScript application is a crucial step in the software development process. Compiling your TypeScript code, setting up a robust testing framework, and writing unit, integration, and end-to-end tests help ensure the reliability, functionality, and performance of your application.

By adopting testing best practices and tools like Jest, Cypress, and others, you can catch and resolve issues early in the development cycle, leading to a more stable and high-quality software product.

BOOK 2
MASTERING TYPESCRIPT ESSENTIALS
ADVANCED CONCEPTS AND PRACTICAL
APPLICATIONS FOR INTERMEDIATE DEVELOPERS

ROB BOTWRIGHT

Chapter 1: Advanced TypeScript Features Overview

As you become more proficient with TypeScript, you'll discover a range of advanced features and techniques that can enhance your code's robustness, maintainability, and expressiveness.

One such feature is Generics, which allows you to write reusable and type-safe code by introducing placeholders for types in functions, classes, and interfaces.

Generics enable you to create functions and data structures that can work with various data types while preserving type information.

For instance, you can define a generic function to swap the positions of two elements in an array:

typescriptCopy code

```
function swap<T>(arr: T[], i: number, j: number): void { const temp = arr[i]; arr[i] = arr[j]; arr[j] = temp; } const numbers = [1, 2, 3, 4]; swap(numbers, 0, 2); // Now numbers = [3, 2, 1, 4] const strings = ['apple', 'banana', 'cherry']; swap(strings, 1, 2); // Now strings = ['apple', 'cherry', 'banana']
```

In this example, the **swap** function uses a generic type parameter **T** to indicate that it can work with arrays of any type. This flexibility allows you to reuse the function with different data types while maintaining type safety.

Generics are invaluable when designing reusable components, such as data structures, algorithms, or higher-order functions, as they enable you to create code that adapts to different data types without sacrificing type checking.

Another advanced TypeScript feature is Decorators, which are a form of metaprogramming that allows you to add metadata or behavior to classes, methods, properties, or parameters.

Decorators are often used in modern web frameworks like Angular and NestJS to configure and extend the behavior of classes and their members.

Here's an example of a decorator that logs method execution:

typescriptCopy code

```
function logMethod(target: any, key: string, descriptor: PropertyDescriptor): PropertyDescriptor {
const originalMethod = descriptor.value;
descriptor.value = function (...args: any[]) {
console.log(`Calling ${key} with arguments: ${JSON.stringify(args)}`); const result = originalMethod.apply(this, args);
console.log(`Method ${key} returned: ${JSON.stringify(result)}`); return result; }; return descriptor; } class Calculator { @logMethod add(a: number, b: number): number { return a + b; } }
const calculator = new Calculator();
calculator.add(3, 5);
```

In this example, the **logMethod** decorator intercepts calls to the **add** method, logs input arguments and the method's return value, and then invokes the original method.

Decorators can be a powerful tool for implementing cross-cutting concerns such as logging, authentication, and validation, making your code more modular and maintainable.

TypeScript also supports Conditional Types, which allow you to express complex type transformations based on conditions. Conditional types use conditional expressions and the **infer** keyword to extract and manipulate types within type definitions.

Here's an example of a conditional type that extracts the parameter types from a function type:

typescriptCopy code

```
type ParameterTypes<T> = T extends (...args: infer P) => any ? P : never; function exampleFunction(a: string, b: number) { return a + b; } type Params = ParameterTypes<typeof exampleFunction>; // Params is [string, number]
```

In this case, the **ParameterTypes** conditional type checks if **T** is a function type and, if so, extracts its parameter types using the **infer** keyword.

Conditional types are particularly useful when working with libraries, frameworks, or APIs that expose complex and nested type structures, allowing you to infer and manipulate types based on various conditions.

Advanced Type Composition is another powerful aspect of TypeScript, where you can combine and transform types using union types, intersection types, mapped types, and more.

Union types allow you to represent values that can be of multiple types, providing flexibility when dealing with diverse data structures:

typescriptCopy code

```
type Result = string | number; const textResult: Result = 'Hello, TypeScript'; const numericResult: Result = 42;
```

Intersection types, on the other hand, allow you to combine multiple types into a single type, capturing all their properties:

typescriptCopy code

```
interface Car { brand: string; year: number; }
interface Engine { type: string; power: number; }
type HybridCar = Car & Engine; const myCar: HybridCar = { brand: 'Toyota', year: 2023, type: 'Electric', power: 150, };
```

Mapped types provide a way to create new types by transforming the properties of an existing type. For example, you can make all properties of an interface optional or readonly using mapped types:

typescriptCopy code

```
interface User { id: number; name: string; email: string; } type PartialUser = { [K in keyof User]?:
```

User[K] }; type ReadonlyUser = { readonly [K in keyof User]: User[K] };

TypeScript's advanced type composition features enable you to model complex data structures and enforce specific constraints, making your code more expressive and maintainable.

Additionally, Advanced Modules and Module Resolution in TypeScript allow you to organize and manage the structure of your project effectively. You can use module systems like CommonJS, ES6 modules, or AMD to encapsulate and modularize your code, improving code maintainability and reusability.

Furthermore, TypeScript's Advanced Error Handling techniques, such as custom error classes and conditional handling, allow you to handle errors gracefully and provide meaningful error messages to users or developers.

By mastering these advanced features in TypeScript, you can write more expressive, modular, and maintainable code, enabling you to tackle complex software development challenges with confidence and precision.

Chapter 2: Type Annotations and Type Inference

Understanding type annotations is fundamental to harnessing the full power of TypeScript, as they allow you to explicitly specify the data types of variables, parameters, and return values in your code.

TypeScript's type system is designed to catch type-related errors at compile-time, providing early feedback on potential issues and enhancing code safety.

In TypeScript, you can annotate variables by using a colon followed by the desired type. For example:

typescriptCopy code

```
let message: string = "Hello, TypeScript!";
```

In this example, the variable **message** is explicitly annotated with the type **string**, indicating that it should only contain string values.

Type annotations are particularly useful when the type of a variable cannot be inferred automatically by TypeScript's type inference system.

For example, when declaring variables without initialization, TypeScript may not be able to determine their types:

typescriptCopy code

```
let age; // No type annotation provided age = 30;
```

In situations like this, adding a type annotation can clarify the intended type:

typescriptCopy code

let age: number; // Type annotation specifies number age = 30;

Type annotations can also be applied to function parameters and return values, ensuring that functions are used correctly and consistently throughout your code.

Consider a simple function that adds two numbers:

typescriptCopy code

```
function addNumbers(a: number, b: number): number { return a + b; }
```

In this function, type annotations specify that both **a** and **b** should be of type **number**, and the function should return a **number**.

Using type annotations in this way helps TypeScript catch errors at compile-time if you attempt to call **addNumbers** with arguments of the wrong type:

typescriptCopy code

```
const result = addNumbers(5, '10'); // Error: Argument of type 'string' is not assignable to parameter of type 'number'.
```

In this example, TypeScript detects that the second argument **'10'** is a string, not a number, and reports an error.

Type annotations are not limited to simple types like **number** and **string**. TypeScript allows you to create custom types using interfaces and define complex type structures.

Interfaces define the structure of objects and can be used as type annotations for variables, function parameters, and return values. For instance:

typescriptCopy code

```
interface Person { name: string; age: number; }
function greet(person: Person): string { return `Hello, ${person.name}! You are ${person.age} years old.`; }
```

In this example, the **Person** interface describes an object with **name** and **age** properties. The **greet** function takes a **Person** as a parameter and returns a string.

TypeScript also supports union types, which allow a variable or parameter to accept multiple types. For instance:

typescriptCopy code

```
let result: number | string; result = 42; // Valid result = 'Hello'; // Valid result = true; // Error: Type 'boolean' is not assignable to type 'number | string'.
```

Here, the **result** variable can be assigned a value of type **number** or **string**, but not **boolean**.

Type annotations can be particularly beneficial when working with arrays and objects. You can specify the types of array elements and object properties using annotations.

For example, you can define an array of numbers and annotate it accordingly:

typescriptCopy code

```
let numbers: number[] = [1, 2, 3, 4];
```

Here, the **numbers** array is annotated to contain only **number** values.

Similarly, you can specify the types of object properties using type annotations:

typescriptCopy code

let person: { name: string; age: number } = { name: 'Alice', age: 30 };

In this case, the **person** object is annotated to have a **name** property of type **string** and an **age** property of type **number**.

TypeScript's type system is powerful and flexible, allowing you to create complex type hierarchies and structures. You can define type aliases and reuse them throughout your code to maintain consistency and readability.

For example, you can define a type alias for a user profile:

typescriptCopy code

type UserProfile = { username: string; email: string; age: number; }; const user: UserProfile = { username: 'jsmith', email: 'jsmith@example.com', age: 25, };

Type annotations are not only useful for enhancing code clarity and safety but also for providing valuable documentation to developers who work with your code. They serve as a form of self-documentation, making it easier for others (and your future self) to understand the expected data types and structures in your codebase.

In addition to variable and function annotations, TypeScript allows you to use type annotations for class properties and methods, enabling comprehensive type checking across your entire application.

TypeScript's type annotations empower you to express your code's intentions clearly and reduce the likelihood of runtime errors. By leveraging this feature effectively, you can write robust, maintainable, and error-free TypeScript code that scales seamlessly as your projects grow in complexity.

Chapter 3: Advanced Functions and Generics

Advanced function patterns in TypeScript allow you to create highly modular, reusable, and expressive code that addresses complex programming challenges.

One such pattern is the use of Higher-Order Functions (HOFs), which are functions that either take other functions as arguments or return functions as their results.

Higher-Order Functions enable you to abstract and encapsulate common behavior, making your code more concise and adaptable.

For example, you can create a generic **map** function that operates on arrays and applies a given function to each element:

typescriptCopy code

```
function map<T, U>(arr: T[], mapper: (item: T) =>
U): U[] { const result: U[] = []; for (const item of arr)
{ result.push(mapper(item)); } return result; } const
numbers = [1, 2, 3, 4]; const doubled =
map(numbers, (n) => n * 2); // [2, 4, 6, 8]
```

In this example, the **map** function takes an array and a mapping function as arguments, and it applies the mapping function to each element of the array.

HOFs like **map** are valuable for abstracting common operations, such as mapping, filtering, and reducing, allowing you to focus on the core logic of your application.

Another advanced function pattern is the use of Closures and Lexical Scoping to create private variables and encapsulate state within functions.

Closures occur when a function "closes over" its lexical environment, capturing variables from its outer scope.

Consider a counter function that uses a closure to maintain its internal state:

typescriptCopy code

```typescript
function createCounter() { let count = 0; return ()
=> { count++; return count; }; } const counter =
createCounter();   console.log(counter());   // 1
console.log(counter()); // 2
```

In this example, the **createCounter** function returns a closure that captures the **count** variable. Each time the closure is invoked, it increments and returns the count.

Closures are a powerful way to encapsulate state and create modular and reusable functions with hidden internal details.

Currying is another advanced function pattern that involves breaking down functions with multiple arguments into a series of single-argument functions.

By currying functions, you can create more flexible and composable code, allowing you to partially apply arguments and create specialized versions of functions.

Here's an example of currying in TypeScript:
typescriptCopy code
```
function curry<T, U, V>(fn: (arg1: T, arg2: U) => V) {
return (arg1: T) => (arg2: U) => fn(arg1, arg2); }
function add(a: number, b: number): number {
return a + b; } const curriedAdd = curry(add); const
addFive = curriedAdd(5); console.log(addFive(3));
// 8
```
In this example, the **curry** function takes a binary
function **fn** and returns a curried version of it. You can
then partially apply arguments to create specialized
functions like **addFive**.

Currying enhances code flexibility and enables the
creation of reusable function pipelines.

Memoization is an advanced function pattern that
involves caching the results of expensive function calls
to improve performance.

Memoization can be particularly valuable in situations
where a function's output depends solely on its input
and doesn't change over time.

Here's a simple memoization example:
typescriptCopy code
```
function memoize<T, U>(fn: (arg: T) => U): (arg: T)
=> U { const cache = new Map<T, U>(); return (arg:
T) => { if (cache.has(arg)) { return cache.get(arg)!; }
else { const result = fn(arg); cache.set(arg, result);
return result; } }; } function fibonacci(n: number):
number { if (n <= 1) { return n; } return fibonacci(n
```

- 1) + fibonacci (n - 2); } const memoizedFibonacci = memoize (fibonacci);

```
console.log(memoizedFibonacci(40)); // Much
```
faster than computing from scratch

In this example, the **memoize** function wraps the expensive **fibonacci** function, caching its results to avoid redundant calculations.

Memoization is a technique to optimize performance by avoiding unnecessary computations, especially in recursive or repetitive function calls.

Composition is an advanced function pattern that involves combining multiple functions to create more complex and expressive functions.

Functional composition allows you to break down complex problems into smaller, composable functions that are easier to reason about and test.

Consider a scenario where you need to transform data by applying multiple operations:

typescriptCopy code

```
function addOne(x: number): number { return x +
1; } function double(x: number): number { return x
* 2; } function square(x: number): number { return
x * x; } const transform = (x: number) =>
square(double(addOne(x)));
```

In this example, the **transform** function applies **addOne**, **double**, and **square** in a specific order to transform the input.

Functional composition allows you to create a more modular and reusable version of the **transform** function:

typescriptCopy code

```typescript
function compose<T, U, V>(f: (x: T) => U, g: (y: U) => V): (x: T) => V { return (x: T) => g(f(x)); } const transform = compose(addOne, compose(double, square));
```

In this refactored code, the **compose** function takes two functions and returns a new function that applies them sequentially. This composition results in a more flexible and maintainable codebase.

Recursion is an advanced function pattern where a function calls itself to solve a problem, making it especially useful for solving problems that involve repetitive or self-similar structures.

For example, you can use recursion to compute the factorial of a number:

typescriptCopy code

```typescript
function factorial(n: number): number { if (n <= 1) { return 1; } else { return n * factorial(n - 1); } }
console.log(factorial(5)); // 120
```

In this recursive **factorial** function, the base case (n <= 1) is defined to terminate the recursion, while the recursive case calculates the factorial by calling the function with a smaller argument.

Recursion is a powerful technique that can simplify complex problems by breaking them down into smaller, manageable subproblems.

The Observer Pattern is an advanced design pattern that allows you to establish one-to-many relationships between objects, where one object (the subject) maintains a list of observers that are notified of changes.

This pattern is commonly used in event-driven systems, user interfaces, and reactive programming.

Here's a simplified example of the Observer Pattern in TypeScript:

```typescript
typescriptCopy code
class Subject { private observers: Observer[] = [];
addObserver(observer: Observer) {
this.observers.push(observer); }
removeObserver(observer: Observer) { const index =
this.observers.indexOf(observer); if (index !== -1) {
this.observers.splice(index, 1); } }
notifyObservers(data: any) { for (const observer of
this.observers) { observer.update(data); } } }
interface Observer { update(data: any): void; }
class ConcreteObserver implements Observer {
update(data: any) { console.log(`Received data:
${data}`); } } const subject = new Subject(); const
observer1 = new ConcreteObserver(); const
observer2 = new ConcreteObserver();
subject.addObserver(observer1);
subject.addObserver(observer2);
```

subject. notifyObservers('Hello, observers!'); // Both observers receive the notification

In this example, the **Subject** maintains a list of observers and notifies them when new data is available. Observers implement the **Observer** interface, which defines the **update** method.

The Observer Pattern promotes loose coupling between subjects and observers, making it an effective way to build extensible and maintainable systems.

Advanced function patterns provide you with powerful tools and techniques to write clean, modular, and expressive code in TypeScript. By mastering these patterns, you can tackle complex programming challenges with confidence and efficiency, while also enhancing the maintainability and readability of your codebase.

Chapter 4: Working with Complex Data Structures

Complex data structures are a fundamental part of software development, enabling you to represent, organize, and manipulate data in sophisticated ways.

In TypeScript, you have access to a variety of complex data structures that can greatly enhance your ability to model and solve real-world problems.

One of the most commonly used complex data structures is the array. An array is an ordered collection of values, and TypeScript provides robust support for working with arrays.

You can declare an array and specify its element type using type annotations:

typescriptCopy code

```
let numbers: number[] = [1, 2, 3, 4, 5];
```

In this example, the **numbers** array contains five elements of type **number**. TypeScript's type system ensures that only numbers can be added to this array.

Arrays offer various methods and operations, such as adding and removing elements, iterating through elements, and searching for specific values.

For example, you can use the **push** method to add elements to the end of an array:

typescriptCopy code

```
numbers.push(6, 7);
```

And you can use the **pop** method to remove the last element:

typescriptCopy code

numbers. pop ();

Additionally, TypeScript supports array methods like **map**, **filter**, and **reduce**, which allow you to perform transformations, filtering, and aggregation on array elements efficiently.

typescriptCopy code

```
const doubled = numbers.map((x) => x * 2); const
evens = numbers.filter((x) => x % 2 === 0); const
sum = numbers.reduce((acc, x) => acc + x, 0);
```

Another complex data structure in TypeScript is the object. Objects are collections of key-value pairs, and they are versatile for representing structured data.

You can define the shape of an object using interfaces or type aliases:

typescriptCopy code

```
interface Person { name: string; age: number; }
const person: Person = { name: 'Alice', age: 30, };
```

In this example, the **Person** interface defines the structure of the **person** object, specifying that it should have a **name** property of type **string** and an **age** property of type **number**.

Objects can also contain nested objects, allowing you to model complex hierarchical data structures:

typescriptCopy code

```
interface Address { street: string; city: string; }
interface UserProfile { username: string; email:
string; address: Address; } const user: UserProfile =
```

{ username: 'jsmith', email: 'jsmith@example.com', address: { street: '123 Main St', city: 'Anytown', }, };
This nested structure illustrates how objects can be used to represent real-world entities and their relationships.

Another essential complex data structure in TypeScript is the Map. Maps are collections of key-value pairs similar to objects, but with some key differences.

Maps can use various data types as keys, including objects, functions, and primitive values, providing more flexibility than objects.

You can create a Map and manipulate it as follows:
typescriptCopy code

```
const userMap = new Map<string, UserProfile>();
userMap.set('jsmith', { username: 'jsmith', email: 'jsmith@example.com', address: { street: '123 Main St', city: 'Anytown', }, }); const userProfile = userMap.get('jsmith');
```

In this example, a Map is used to associate usernames with user profiles. The **set** method adds a key-value pair to the Map, and the **get** method retrieves the value associated with a specific key.

Maps are particularly useful when you need to maintain the order of key-value pairs or when you require more control over key types.

Additionally, TypeScript provides Sets, which are collections of unique values. Sets are useful for efficiently managing distinct elements, removing duplicates, and performing set operations.

You can create a Set and manipulate it as follows:

typescriptCopy code

```
const uniqueNumbers = new Set<number>();
uniqueNumbers.add(1); uniqueNumbers.add(2);
uniqueNumbers.add(2); // Ignored because it's a duplicate const containsTwo = uniqueNumbers.has(2); // true
```

In this example, the Set **uniqueNumbers** ensures that duplicate values are automatically filtered out, and the **has** method checks if a specific value is present in the Set.

Sets are an excellent choice when you need to work with collections of distinct elements.

One of the most powerful and flexible complex data structures in TypeScript is the class. Classes allow you to define custom data structures with properties and methods, encapsulating both data and behavior.

You can create classes to model real-world entities, abstract concepts, or custom data types:

typescriptCopy code

```
class Point { x: number; y: number; constructor(x: number, y: number) { this.x = x; this.y = y; } distanceToOrigin(): number { return Math.sqrt(this.x ** 2 + this.y ** 2); }} const point = new Point(3, 4); console.log(point.distanceToOrigin()); // 5
```

In this example, the **Point** class represents a point in a 2D space. It has properties **x** and **y**, a constructor to initialize those properties, and a method **distanceToOrigin** that calculates the distance from the point to the origin. Classes are a powerful way to create custom data structures and reusable components in TypeScript. Lastly, TypeScript supports the use of Enums, which are a way to define a set of named constant values. Enums are particularly useful when you have a fixed set of values that represent distinct options or states. Here's an example:

typescriptCopy code

```
enum Color { Red, Green, Blue, } const selectedColor = Color.Green;
```

In this case, the **Color** enum defines three constant values: **Red**, **Green**, and **Blue**. You can use these values to represent colors in a way that's both readable and type-safe. Enums are especially beneficial in scenarios where you want to avoid "magic strings" and ensure that specific values conform to a predefined set of options. In summary, complex data structures in TypeScript, such as arrays, objects, maps, sets, classes, and enums, empower you to represent and manipulate data in diverse and powerful ways. By understanding how to use these data structures effectively, you can design more efficient algorithms, create modular and reusable code, and model complex real-world scenarios with confidence.

Chapter 5: Asynchronous Programming with Promises and Async/Await

Managing concurrency in software development is a critical aspect of building efficient and responsive applications.

Concurrency allows multiple tasks to execute independently and potentially in parallel, enabling your applications to make the most of available resources and provide a smoother user experience.

One common challenge in concurrent programming is handling asynchronous operations, such as network requests, file I/O, or user interactions, without blocking the main thread of execution.

Blocking the main thread can lead to unresponsive applications, frustrating users, and degrading the overall performance of your software.

To address these challenges, JavaScript introduced Promises, a powerful abstraction for managing asynchronous operations.

Promises provide a structured way to work with asynchronous tasks, making it easier to handle their outcomes and coordinate multiple operations.

A Promise represents a value that might be available now, in the future, or never. It has three states: pending, fulfilled, or rejected.

A Promise is typically created by invoking a function that performs an asynchronous operation and returns a Promise object.

For example, consider a function that fetches data from a remote server using the Fetch API:

typescriptCopy code

```
function fetchData() { return fetch('https://api.example.com/data')
.then((response) => { if (!response.ok) { throw new Error('Network request failed'); } return response.json(); }) .then((data) => { // Process the retrieved data return data; }) .catch((error) => { // Handle errors console.error(error); }); }
```

In this example, the **fetchData** function returns a Promise that fetches data from the specified URL, processes it, and handles any errors that may occur during the network request.

Using Promises, you can perform asynchronous tasks and respond to their completion or failure by attaching **.then()** and **.catch()** handlers to the Promise.

Promises provide a structured way to compose and sequence asynchronous operations, making it easier to reason about your code and manage concurrency effectively.

While Promises are a significant improvement over traditional callback-based asynchronous programming, JavaScript introduced Async/Await to simplify asynchronous code even further.

Async/Await is a language feature that allows you to write asynchronous code in a more synchronous and linear style, making it easier to understand and maintain.

With Async/Await, you can write asynchronous functions that look like regular synchronous functions, using the **async** keyword before the function declaration and **await** within the function body.

Here's an example of using Async/Await to rewrite the previous **fetchData** function:

typescriptCopy code

```
async function fetchData() { try { const response = await fetch('https://api.example.com/data'); if (!response.ok) { throw new Error('Network request failed'); } const data = await response.json(); // Process the retrieved data return data; } catch (error) { // Handle errors console.error(error); } }
```

In this refactored code, the **async** keyword is used to define an asynchronous function, and the **await** keyword is used to pause the execution of the function until the asynchronous operation is completed.

Using Async/Await, you can eliminate callback hell and create more readable and maintainable asynchronous code.

Another advantage of Async/Await is that it allows you to use standard control flow constructs like **try** and **catch** for error handling, making it easier to handle and propagate errors in asynchronous operations.

Furthermore, Async/Await simplifies the process of parallelizing multiple asynchronous operations, also known as concurrent programming.

You can use **Promise.all()** with Async/Await to wait for multiple Promises to resolve concurrently and collect their results:

typescriptCopy code

```
async function fetchMultipleData() { const promise1 = fetchData('https://api.example.com/data1'); const promise2 = fetchData('https://api.example.com/data2'); try { const [data1, data2] = await Promise.all([promise1, promise2]); // Process data1 and data2 concurrently return [data1, data2]; } catch (error) { // Handle errors console.error(error); } }
```

In this example, **fetchMultipleData** asynchronously fetches data from two different URLs concurrently using **await** and **Promise.all()**.

By leveraging Async/Await and Promises, you can write concise and efficient code that effectively manages concurrency and provides a responsive user experience.

It's important to note that while Promises and Async/Await simplify asynchronous programming, you still need to consider error handling, resource management, and performance optimization when working with concurrent operations.

Additionally, be cautious about overusing concurrency, as excessive parallelism can lead to resource contention and negatively impact application performance.

To optimize the concurrency in your application, consider techniques such as throttling, debouncing, and load balancing, depending on your specific requirements.

In summary, managing concurrency with Promises and Async/Await is a fundamental skill for building modern, responsive, and efficient applications in JavaScript and TypeScript.

These features provide a structured and readable way to work with asynchronous operations, making it easier to handle errors, compose complex workflows, and parallelize tasks.

By mastering Promises and Async/Await, you can confidently develop applications that leverage the full potential of concurrent programming while ensuring a smooth user experience.

Chapter 6: Advanced Object-Oriented Programming in TypeScript

Advanced class and interface concepts in TypeScript empower developers to create highly structured and modular code, facilitating the construction of complex and maintainable software systems.

Next, we will explore various advanced techniques and best practices for working with classes and interfaces in TypeScript.

One of the fundamental concepts in object-oriented programming is inheritance, and TypeScript provides robust support for creating class hierarchies through inheritance.

Inheritance allows you to define a base class with common properties and methods, and then create derived classes that inherit and extend the behavior of the base class.

For instance, consider a base class **Animal** with properties like **name** and **age** and a method **makeSound**:

typescriptCopy code

```
class Animal { name: string; age: number;
constructor(name: string, age: number) { this.name
= name; this.age = age; } makeSound() {
console.log("Animal makes a sound"); } }
```

You can then create derived classes like **Dog** and **Cat** that inherit from the **Animal** class:

typescriptCopy code

```
class Dog extends Animal { constructor(name:
string, age: number) { super(name, age); }
makeSound() { console.log("Dog barks"); } } class
Cat extends Animal { constructor(name: string, age:
number) { super(name, age); } makeSound() {
console.log("Cat meows"); } }
```

In this example, **Dog** and **Cat** inherit the properties and methods of **Animal** while providing their own implementations of the **makeSound** method.

Inheritance is a powerful mechanism for code reuse and creating class hierarchies, but it should be used judiciously to avoid tight coupling between classes and to favor composition when possible.

Another key concept in class-based programming is encapsulation, which refers to the practice of hiding internal details of a class and exposing a well-defined interface to the outside world.

In TypeScript, you can achieve encapsulation by using access modifiers like **public, private**, and **protected**.

The **public** access modifier is the default and allows unrestricted access to class members:

typescriptCopy code

```
class MyClass { publicProperty: string;
constructor(publicProperty: string) {
this.publicProperty = publicProperty; } }
```

The **private** access modifier restricts access to class members only within the class:

typescriptCopy code

```
class MyClass { private privateProperty: string;
constructor(privateProperty: string) {
this.privateProperty = privateProperty; } }
```

The **protected** access modifier is similar to **private**, but it allows access from derived classes:

typescriptCopy code

```
class BaseClass { protected protectedProperty:
string; constructor(protectedProperty: string) {
this.protectedProperty = protectedProperty; } } class
DerivedClass extends BaseClass {
constructor(protectedProperty: string) {
super(protectedProperty); } getProtectedProperty() {
return this.protectedProperty; } }
```

Encapsulation helps maintain class integrity and prevents unintended modification of internal state. It also enables controlled access to class members and facilitates changes to the class's implementation without affecting its consumers.

Interfaces play a crucial role in TypeScript's type system, allowing you to define contracts for classes and objects to adhere to.

An interface defines a set of properties and methods that a class must implement to be considered an instance of that interface.

For example, consider an interface **Shape** that defines a method **calculateArea**:

typescriptCopy code

```
interface Shape { calculateArea(): number; }
```

You can then create classes like **Circle** and **Rectangle** that implement the **Shape** interface:

typescriptCopy code

```
class Circle implements Shape { constructor(private radius: number) {} calculateArea() { return Math.PI * this.radius ** 2; } } class Rectangle implements Shape { constructor(private width: number, private height: number) {} calculateArea() { return this.width * this.height; } }
```

By implementing the **calculateArea** method, these classes fulfill the contract defined by the **Shape** interface.

Interfaces provide a powerful way to define the shape of objects and ensure that classes adhere to specific contracts, making your code more robust and predictable.

Advanced TypeScript features like intersection types and union types allow you to create more flexible and expressive interfaces.

Intersection types combine multiple types into a single type, allowing an object to have properties and methods from multiple sources.

For example, you can define an **Editable** interface that represents objects with both **edit** and **save** methods:

typescriptCopy code

```typescript
interface Editable { edit(): void; } interface Savable
{ save(): void; } type EditableAndSavable = Editable
& Savable; class Document implements
EditableAndSavable { edit() { console.log("Editing
document"); } save() { console.log("Saving
document"); } }
```

In this example, the **EditableAndSavable** type combines the **Editable** and **Savable** interfaces, ensuring that classes implementing it have both **edit** and **save** methods.

Union types, on the other hand, allow a variable or parameter to accept values of multiple types.

Consider a function that accepts either a **string** or an **number**:

typescriptCopy code

```typescript
function printValue(value: string | number) {
console.log(value); } printValue("Hello,
TypeScript!"); // Outputs: Hello, TypeScript!
printValue(42); // Outputs: 42
```

Union types provide flexibility when working with diverse data types and enable you to write more generic and reusable code.

TypeScript also supports abstract classes, which are classes that cannot be instantiated directly but serve as base classes for other classes.

Abstract classes are used to define a common interface and behavior that derived classes must implement.

For instance, you can create an abstract class **Shape** with an abstract method **calculateArea**:

typescriptCopy code

```typescript
abstract class Shape { abstract calculateArea(): number; } class Circle extends Shape { constructor(private radius: number) { super(); } calculateArea() { return Math.PI * this.radius ** 2; } } class Rectangle extends Shape { constructor(private width: number, private height: number) { super(); } calculateArea() { return this.width * this.height; } }
```

In this example, **Shape** is an abstract class with the abstract method **calculateArea**, and **Circle** and **Rectangle** are derived classes that implement this method.

Abstract classes enforce a contract for derived classes, ensuring that they provide specific behavior.

Advanced class and interface concepts in TypeScript enable you to design sophisticated and maintainable software systems.

By leveraging inheritance, encapsulation, and interfaces, you can create well-structured and modular code that adheres to defined contracts and promotes code reuse.

Intersection and union types offer flexibility and expressiveness when defining interfaces, and abstract classes provide a mechanism for enforcing common behavior in derived classes.

Understanding and applying these advanced concepts will empower you to build robust and scalable TypeScript applications.

Chapter 7: Decorators and Metaprogramming

Metaprogramming is a powerful technique that allows you to write code that can analyze, generate, modify, or manipulate other code at runtime.

In TypeScript, metaprogramming can be used to create more flexible and dynamic software, automate repetitive tasks, and build advanced libraries and frameworks.

One of the fundamental tools for metaprogramming in TypeScript is the ability to work with the type system.

TypeScript's type system is designed to be expressive and extensible, allowing you to define complex types, generics, and type aliases to capture specific patterns and structures in your code.

By leveraging the type system, you can create generic functions and classes that work with a wide range of types, making your code more reusable and adaptable.

For example, consider a generic function that swaps the values of two variables:

typescriptCopy code

```
function swap<T>(a: T, b: T): [T, T] { return [b, a]; }
const [x, y] = swap(10, 20); const [str1, str2] = swap("Hello", "World");
```

In this example, the **swap** function is generic, meaning it can work with any type **T**. The type parameter **T** allows TypeScript to infer the correct types for **x**, **y**, **str1**, and **str2**.

This type of metaprogramming enables you to create versatile and type-safe functions and classes that adapt to various data types.

Another metaprogramming technique in TypeScript involves using decorators.

Decorators are a form of metaprogramming that allows you to add metadata and behavior to classes, methods, and properties at compile time.

You can create custom decorators to extend the functionality of your classes or apply existing decorators from libraries and frameworks.

For example, consider a simple class decorator that logs when a class is instantiated:

typescriptCopy code

```
function logClass(target: Function) {
console.log(`Class ${target.name} has been
instantiated.`); } @logClass class MyClass {
constructor() {} } const instance = new MyClass(); //
Outputs: Class MyClass has been instantiated.
```

In this example, the **logClass** decorator logs a message when an instance of the decorated class is created.

Decorators can be used for a wide range of purposes, such as adding validation logic, implementing aspect-oriented programming, or integrating with third-party libraries.

They provide a powerful mechanism for extending and modifying class behavior without directly altering the class's code.

Additionally, TypeScript allows you to work with metadata reflection, which enables you to inspect and manipulate class and method metadata at runtime.

To access metadata, you can use the **Reflect** object, which provides methods like **Reflect.getMetadata** and **Reflect.defineMetadata**.

For instance, consider a scenario where you want to store and retrieve metadata about class properties:

typescriptCopy code

```
class MyClass { @Reflect.metadata("description",
"This is a property") myProperty: string = ""; } const
description = Reflect.getMetadata("description",
MyClass.prototype,                    "myProperty");
console.log(description); // Outputs: This is a
property
```

In this example, the **@Reflect.metadata** decorator is used to attach metadata to the **myProperty** class property. Later, the **Reflect.getMetadata** method is used to retrieve the metadata associated with that property.

This reflective metaprogramming allows you to build powerful frameworks, libraries, and tools that can introspect and manipulate code structures at runtime.

TypeScript also provides a feature called template literals, which allows you to embed expressions within string literals using backticks (`).

Template literals offer a powerful way to perform string interpolation, making it easier to generate dynamic strings and code.

For instance, you can use template literals to generate SQL queries with dynamic parameters:

typescriptCopy code

```
function generateSQLQuery(name: string, age: number) { return `SELECT * FROM users WHERE name = '${name}' AND age = ${age}`; } const sqlQuery = generateSQLQuery("Alice", 30); console.log(sqlQuery);
```

In this example, the **generateSQLQuery** function uses template literals to create a SQL query string with dynamic values.

Template literals are particularly useful for generating code snippets, generating dynamic configuration files, or constructing complex strings based on runtime data.

Another advanced metaprogramming technique in TypeScript is code generation.

Code generation involves creating code at runtime to achieve specific tasks, such as generating API clients, serialization code, or configuration files.

For instance, you can create a code generator that generates TypeScript interfaces based on JSON data:

typescriptCopy code

```
function generateInterfaceFromJSON(jsonData: string, interfaceName: string) { const data = JSON.parse(jsonData); let interfaceCode = `interface
```

```
${interfaceName} {\n`; for (const key in data) { if
(data.hasOwnProperty(key)) { const valueType =
typeof data[key]; interfaceCode += ` ${key}:
${valueType};\n`; } } interfaceCode += "}\n"; return
interfaceCode; } const jsonData = '{"name": "Alice",
"age": 30}'; const interfaceCode =
generateInterfaceFromJSON(jsonData, "Person");
console.log(interfaceCode);
```

In this example, the **generateInterfaceFromJSON**
function takes JSON data and an interface name as
input and generates TypeScript code for an interface
that matches the data structure.

Code generation can significantly reduce manual
work, improve code quality, and ensure consistency
when dealing with repetitive or boilerplate code.

Furthermore, TypeScript allows you to create custom
transformers, which are plugins that can modify the
abstract syntax tree (AST) of your TypeScript code
during compilation.

Custom transformers provide fine-grained control
over the code transformation process and enable
advanced metaprogramming scenarios.

For instance, you can create a custom transformer to
automatically generate code documentation based on
comments and JSDoc annotations in your code:

typescriptCopy code

```
// @generate-docs class MyClass { /** * This
method does something important. * @param value -
The input value. * @returns The result. */
```

```
myMethod(value: number): number { return value
* 2; } }
```

In this example, the **@generate-docs** comment is used to indicate that the custom transformer should generate documentation for the **MyClass** class and its **myMethod** method.

Custom transformers offer a powerful way to automate code transformations, enforce coding standards, or perform advanced code analysis.

In summary, metaprogramming techniques in TypeScript provide developers with powerful tools for creating dynamic and flexible software.

By leveraging the type system, decorators, metadata reflection, template literals, code generation, and custom transformers, you can build more reusable, maintainable, and extensible code.

Metaprogramming allows you to automate repetitive tasks, create sophisticated libraries and frameworks, and adapt your code to changing requirements with ease.

Chapter 8: Building Modular Applications with TypeScript

Dependency Injection (DI) and Inversion of Control (IoC) are two closely related design principles that play a significant role in creating modular, testable, and maintainable software.

These principles are widely used in modern software development, including TypeScript, to manage dependencies, enhance code flexibility, and improve code quality.

At their core, Dependency Injection and Inversion of Control address the problem of how to provide a component with the objects it depends on without creating tight coupling between components.

In traditional programming, objects often create and manage their own dependencies directly, resulting in rigid and tightly coupled code.

Dependency Injection solves this problem by allowing dependencies to be injected into a component from an external source, typically through constructor parameters or property setters.

This external source is often referred to as an Inversion of Control container, which manages the creation and lifetime of objects.

Consider a TypeScript class that represents a service for sending emails. In a non-DI scenario, the class might directly instantiate its dependencies, like an SMTP client:

typescriptCopy code

```
class EmailService { private smtpClient: SmtpClient;
constructor() { this.smtpClient = new SmtpClient();
} sendEmail(to: string, subject: string, message:
string): void { // Logic for sending the email using
this.smtpClient } }
```

In this example, the **EmailService** class tightly couples itself to the **SmtpClient**, making it challenging to substitute or mock the **SmtpClient** for testing or switching to a different implementation.

However, with Dependency Injection, you can rewrite the **EmailService** to accept its dependencies through the constructor:

typescriptCopy code

```
class EmailService { constructor(private smtpClient:
SmtpClient) {} sendEmail(to: string, subject: string,
message: string): void { // Logic for sending the
email using this.smtpClient } }
```

Now, the **EmailService** class relies on an external source (the injected **SmtpClient**) to fulfill its dependencies, adhering to the Dependency Injection principle.

This change improves the flexibility of the **EmailService** class because you can inject different implementations of **SmtpClient** or mock it for testing purposes.

Inversion of Control (IoC) takes Dependency Injection a step further by introducing a container or framework that manages the lifecycle and resolution of dependencies.

The IoC container is responsible for instantiating and wiring together the various components of an application, ensuring that they receive the correct dependencies when needed.

One common use case for IoC containers in TypeScript is in web application frameworks like Angular or NestJS.

These frameworks provide a built-in IoC container that manages the instantiation and dependency injection of components, such as controllers, services, and modules.

For instance, in Angular, you can define a service and inject it into a component like this:

typescriptCopy code

```
@Injectable() class MyService { // Service logic }
@Component({ selector: 'app-my-component',
template: '<div>{{ myServiceData }}</div>', }) class
MyComponent { constructor(private myService:
MyService) {} }
```

In this example, the Angular framework's IoC container automatically resolves and injects the **MyService** dependency into the **MyComponent** class.

Using an IoC container simplifies the management of dependencies and promotes a modular and testable codebase.

However, Dependency Injection and Inversion of Control are not limited to frameworks and can be applied in any TypeScript project.

You can create your own IoC container or use existing libraries like **inversify**, **tsyringe**, or **awilix** to manage dependencies.

Additionally, TypeScript's static type checking provides added benefits when working with Dependency Injection, as it helps catch dependency-related errors at compile time.

To create an IoC container in TypeScript manually, you can define classes for your services and use constructor injection to provide dependencies.

Here's a simple example:

typescriptCopy code

```
class Logger { log(message: string): void {
console.log(message); } } class MyService {
constructor(private logger: Logger) {}
doSomething(): void { this.logger.log('Doing
something...'); } } const logger = new Logger(); const
myService = new MyService(logger);
myService.doSomething(); // Outputs: Doing
something...
```

In this example, the **MyService** class relies on the **Logger** class for logging, and we manually create instances and wire them together.

While manual dependency injection can work for small projects, using an IoC container becomes more beneficial as your application grows in complexity.

IoC containers provide a centralized way to manage dependencies, enabling features like component resolution, dependency lifecycle management, and easy configuration.

When building larger-scale TypeScript applications, you'll often encounter scenarios where you need to manage complex dependencies and handle service registration, scoping, and resolution.

Using an IoC container simplifies these challenges and promotes the principles of Dependency Injection and Inversion of Control.

Another advantage of Dependency Injection and Inversion of Control is improved testability.

By injecting dependencies, you can easily substitute them with mock objects or stubs during testing, allowing you to isolate and test individual components of your application.

For example, when testing the **EmailService** from earlier, you can provide a mock **SmtpClient** instead of a real one to ensure that the service behaves as expected without sending actual emails.

typescriptCopy code

```typescript
class MockSmtpClient {} describe('EmailService', ()
=> { it('should send an email', () => { const
mockSmtpClient = new MockSmtpClient(); const
emailService = new EmailService(mockSmtpClient);
// Test the behavior of sending an email }); });
```

This approach allows you to write unit tests with controlled dependencies, ensuring that each component behaves correctly in isolation.

In summary, Dependency Injection and Inversion of Control are fundamental principles in modern software development, including TypeScript.

They promote modular, flexible, and testable code by decoupling components and managing dependencies in a controlled and centralized manner.

By applying these principles and using IoC containers, you can improve the maintainability, scalability, and testability of your TypeScript applications, leading to higher code quality and developer productivity.

Chapter 9: Integrating TypeScript with Popular Libraries and Frameworks

TypeScript and React are two powerful technologies that, when combined, offer a robust and efficient way to build modern web applications.

React, developed and maintained by Facebook, is a popular JavaScript library for building user interfaces.

TypeScript, on the other hand, is a statically typed superset of JavaScript that provides enhanced tooling and type safety.

In this comprehensive guide, we'll explore how TypeScript can be used effectively with React to create scalable and maintainable applications.

React is known for its component-based architecture, which allows developers to build UIs by composing reusable and self-contained components.

When using TypeScript with React, the first step is to set up your development environment.

You can start a new React project with TypeScript by using the Create React App tool, which simplifies the setup process.

To create a new TypeScript-based React app, open your terminal and run the following command:

bashCopy code

```
npx create-react-app my-ts-react-app --template typescript
```

This command creates a new React project called "my-ts-react-app" with TypeScript configuration preconfigured.

Once your project is set up, you can start building React components with TypeScript.

In TypeScript, you'll often work with interfaces to define the shape of your data.

For instance, if you have a component that receives props with a specific structure, you can define an interface for those props:

typescriptCopy code

```
interface MyComponentProps { name: string; age:
number; } const MyComponent:
React.FC<MyComponentProps> = ({ name, age }) =>
{ return ( <div> <p>Name: {name}</p> <p>Age:
{age}</p> </div> ); };
```

By defining the **MyComponentProps** interface, you provide clear documentation and type safety for the props that **MyComponent** expects to receive.

This is especially useful in large-scale applications where code readability and maintainability are crucial.

TypeScript also helps catch potential issues at compile time, such as passing incorrect prop types to components.

Another essential aspect of using TypeScript with React is managing state in your components.

React provides hooks like **useState** and **useReducer** for managing component state, and TypeScript can help ensure that your state management is type-safe.

For example, if you're using **useState** to manage a boolean state variable, you can explicitly specify the type of the state variable:

typescriptCopy code

```
const [isActive, setIsActive] = useState<boolean>(false);
```

This ensures that **isActive** can only be a boolean value, reducing the likelihood of runtime errors.

In addition to managing component state, you may encounter scenarios where you need to manage global state in your React application.

Popular libraries like Redux and Mobx can be integrated seamlessly with TypeScript to provide predictable state management.

For instance, when using Redux, you can create type-safe action creators and reducers:

typescriptCopy code

```
// Define action types enum ActionTypes { INCREMENT = 'INCREMENT', DECREMENT = 'DECREMENT', } // Define action creators with type annotations const increment = (): { type: ActionTypes.INCREMENT } => ({ type: ActionTypes.INCREMENT, }); const decrement = (): { type: ActionTypes.DECREMENT } => ({ type: ActionTypes.DECREMENT, }); // Define the reducer with type annotations const counterReducer = ( state: number = 0, action: { type: ActionTypes } ): number => { switch (action.type) { case
```

ActionTypes.INCREMENT: return state + 1; case ActionTypes.DECREMENT: return state - 1; default: return state; } };

By using TypeScript, you can ensure that action creators and reducers are type-safe, preventing runtime errors due to incorrect action types.

When working with React, you'll often render lists of items, and TypeScript can assist you in handling these scenarios with type safety.

Consider a component that renders a list of user names:

typescriptCopy code

```typescript
interface User { id: number; name: string; } const UserList: React.FC<{ users: User[] }> = ({ users }) => { return ( <ul> {users.map((user) => ( <li key={user.id}>{user.name}</li> ))} </ul> ); };
```

By specifying that the **UserList** component expects an array of **User** objects as props, TypeScript ensures that you provide the correct data structure when using the component.

Furthermore, TypeScript can help with more complex scenarios, such as handling form inputs and submitting data to a server.

When creating forms in React, you can define interfaces for the form's state and handle form submissions with type-safe code:

typescriptCopy code

```typescript
interface FormData { username: string; password: string; } const LoginForm: React.FC = () => { const
```

```
[formData, setFormData] = useState<FormData>({
username: '', password: '', }); const handleChange
= (e: React.ChangeEvent<HTMLInputElement>) => {
const { name, value } = e.target; setFormData({
...formData, [name]: value }); }; const handleSubmit
= (e: React.FormEvent<HTMLFormElement>) => {
e.preventDefault(); // Submit formData to the server
}; return ( <form onSubmit={handleSubmit}> <input
type="text"                        name="username"
value={formData.username}
onChange={handleChange}        />        <input
type="password"                    name="password"
value={formData.password}
onChange={handleChange}        />        <button
type="submit">Submit</button> </form> ); };
```

In this example, TypeScript ensures that the
handleChange function correctly updates the
formData state and that the form fields are
associated with the correct properties.

This type safety can be especially valuable when
handling complex forms with many fields and
validation requirements.

Additionally, TypeScript can help you create and
consume reusable components in your React
application.

By defining and exporting TypeScript interfaces for
your component props, you provide clear

documentation for component users and ensure that they provide the correct props.

For example, if you create a reusable **Button** component, you can define an interface for its props like this:

typescriptCopy code

```
interface ButtonProps { label: string; onClick: () => void; } const Button: React.FC<ButtonProps> = ({ label, onClick }) => { return <button onClick={onClick}>{label}</button>; }; export default Button;
```

Now, when other developers use your **Button** component, TypeScript will guide them to provide the required **label** and **onClick** props, ensuring that the component behaves as expected.

Moreover, TypeScript can help you document and enforce the usage of context in your React application.

React's context API allows you to share state or functionality between components without having to pass props manually through multiple levels of the component tree.

By creating TypeScript interfaces for your context values, you can provide clear type information and prevent runtime errors.

Consider a scenario where you have a theme context that provides a theme object to child components:

typescriptCopy code

```typescript
interface Theme { backgroundColor: string;
textColor: string; } interface ThemeContextValue {
theme: Theme; toggleTheme: () => void; } const
ThemeContext                                    =
React.createContext<ThemeContextValue          |
undefined>(undefined);     const    ThemeProvider:
React.FC  =  ({  children })  =>  {  const  [theme,
setTheme] = useState<Theme>({ backgroundColor:
'white', textColor: 'black', }); const toggleTheme = ()
=>  {  //  Toggle  theme  logic  };  return  (
<ThemeContext.Provider        value={{        theme,
toggleTheme             }}>             {children}
</ThemeContext.Provider> ); };
```

In this example, TypeScript ensures that the
ThemeContext value provided by the **ThemeProvider**
contains the correct properties (**theme** and
toggleTheme), and components consuming the
context will receive type-checked values.

Furthermore, TypeScript's type inference can help
improve the readability and maintainability of your
React code.

When defining components and their props,
TypeScript can infer types based on the values and
functions you use.

For example, if you create a component that receives
an array of strings as props and maps over them to
render a list, TypeScript can infer the type of the
props, making your code more concise:

typescriptCopy code

```typescript
const StringList: React.FC<{ items: string[] }> = ({ items }) => { return ( <ul> {items.map((item, index) => ( <li key={index}>{item}</li> ))} </ul> ); };
```

TypeScript's inference capabilities reduce the need for explicit type annotations, making your code easier to write and maintain.

When working with TypeScript and React, it's also essential to understand how to manage external libraries and third-party components.

Many popular React libraries and UI frameworks provide TypeScript typings, allowing you to leverage type-safe features and integrate them seamlessly into your application.

For instance, if you're using Material-UI, a popular React UI framework, you can install the TypeScript typings package:

bashCopy code

```bash
npm install @mui/material @mui/icons-material @types/material-ui -D
```

Once you have the typings in place, you can use Material-UI components with TypeScript and benefit from auto-completion and type checking:

typescriptCopy code

```typescript
import React from 'react'; import Button from '@mui/material/Button'; const MyComponent: React.FC = () => { return ( <Button variant="contained" color="primary"> Click Me </Button> ); };
```

By following TypeScript best practices and leveraging typings for third-party libraries, you can create more reliable and maintainable React applications.

Furthermore, TypeScript can be valuable when working on large-scale React projects with multiple developers.

TypeScript's static type checking helps catch errors early, reducing the chances of runtime issues and improving collaboration among team members.

For example, when multiple developers work on different parts of a React application, TypeScript's type annotations and interfaces provide a common understanding of data structures and function signatures. This shared understanding leads to better communication and smoother integration of components. TypeScript also offers features like code navigation and code completion, which enhance the development experience when working with large codebases.

Developers can easily explore the structure of the code, find references, and receive helpful hints about available properties and methods.

These features contribute to increased productivity and a better development experience.

In addition to type safety and tooling improvements, TypeScript offers robust support for modern JavaScript features.

TypeScript's compatibility with ES6 and beyond allows you to take advantage of the latest JavaScript capabilities while ensuring code correctness.

For example, you can use features like arrow functions, destructuring, async/await, and classes in your React components with TypeScript without compatibility issues.

TypeScript also supports JSX, the syntax extension used by React for defining component structures within JavaScript or TypeScript code.

When working with JSX in TypeScript, you'll often use TypeScript's **.tsx** file extension to indicate that the file contains both TypeScript and JSX code.

This allows TypeScript to understand and type-check JSX elements and expressions, ensuring that your React components are correctly written.

In summary, TypeScript and React complement each other seamlessly, offering a robust and efficient way to build modern web applications.

TypeScript enhances React development by providing static type checking, improved tooling, and a more reliable development experience.

By using TypeScript with React, you can create scalable and maintainable applications, benefit from type safety, and harness the full power of React's component-based architecture.

Whether you're building a small project or a large-scale application, TypeScript and React together provide a powerful combination for web development.

Chapter 10: Real-World Projects and Best Practices

Scalability is a critical consideration when developing TypeScript projects, as it ensures that your codebase can grow and evolve over time without becoming unmanageable.

Next, we'll explore best practices for building scalable TypeScript projects that can handle increasing complexity and size.

One of the fundamental practices for scalability in TypeScript projects is organizing your codebase effectively.

To achieve this, it's essential to structure your project into meaningful directories and files.

A common directory structure for TypeScript projects includes folders like "src" for source code, "tests" for tests, and "dist" for compiled output.

Within the "src" folder, you can further organize your code into modules or feature-specific directories.

For instance, you might have a "components" directory for React components, a "utils" directory for utility functions, and a "services" directory for data-fetching services.

This organized structure makes it easier to locate and maintain specific pieces of code as your project grows.

Furthermore, TypeScript provides the ability to define custom module aliases, improving code readability and maintainability.

By configuring module aliases in your TypeScript project, you can use shorter and more descriptive import paths.

For example, instead of importing a module like this:

typescriptCopy code

```
import { someFunction } from '../../utils/myUtil';
```

You can create an alias and use it like this:

typescriptCopy code

```
import { someFunction } from '@myapp/utils/myUtil';
```

To set up module aliases in your TypeScript project, you can use the "paths" configuration in your "tsconfig.json" file:

jsonCopy code

```
{ "compilerOptions": { "baseUrl": "./", "paths": { "@myapp/*": ["src/*"] } } }
```

In this example, we define the "@myapp/" *alias, which maps to the "src/"* directory.

Using aliases not only improves code readability but also simplifies refactoring and makes it easier to move files around without updating import paths manually.

Another crucial aspect of building scalable TypeScript projects is utilizing TypeScript's static type system effectively.

TypeScript's type checking helps catch errors at compile time, reducing the likelihood of runtime issues.

To make the most of TypeScript's type system, it's essential to provide accurate type annotations for your code.

This includes specifying types for function parameters, return values, and variable declarations.

Additionally, TypeScript offers built-in utility types, such as "Partial," "Required," and "Record," that can simplify type definitions and make your code more concise.

For example, if you have a function that expects an object with specific properties but wants to allow some of them to be optional, you can use the "Partial" utility type:

typescriptCopy code

```
interface MyOptions { option1: string; option2: number; option3: boolean; } function configure(options: Partial<MyOptions>): void { // Configure based on options }
```

By utilizing utility types like "Partial," you can express your intentions clearly and concisely.

Another TypeScript feature that contributes to scalability is the ability to work with generics.

Generics allow you to write reusable code that can work with different types while maintaining type safety.

For instance, you can create a generic function to find the maximum value in an array of any type:

typescriptCopy code

```
function findMax<T>(array: T[]): T | undefined { if
(array.length === 0) { return undefined; } let max =
array[0]; for (const item of array) { if (item > max) {
max = item; } } return max; }
```

This "findMax" function works with arrays of numbers, strings, or any other type, and TypeScript ensures that the result is of the same type as the elements in the array.

Generics enable you to write flexible and reusable code that adapts to different data types, making your project more scalable.

When working on scalable TypeScript projects, consider the importance of automated testing.

Automated testing helps ensure that your code functions correctly and continues to work as you make changes or add new features.

In TypeScript projects, you can write unit tests using testing frameworks like Jest, Mocha, or Jasmine.

These frameworks provide utilities for writing and running tests, as well as built-in assertion libraries for making test assertions.

To get started with Jest, you can install it as a development dependency in your project:

bashCopy code

```
npm install jest @types/jest --save-dev
```

Next, you can create test files with the ".test.ts" or ".spec.ts" file extensions to indicate that they contain tests.

For example, if you have a utility function called "sum," you can write a test for it like this:

typescriptCopy code

```typescript
// sum.ts function sum(a: number, b: number): number { return a + b; } export default sum;
```

typescriptCopy code

```typescript
// sum.test.ts import sum from './sum'; test('adds 1 + 2 to equal 3', () => { expect(sum(1, 2)).toBe(3); });
```

By writing tests, you ensure that your code functions correctly, and any regressions are caught early.

Additionally, consider implementing continuous integration (CI) and continuous delivery (CD) pipelines in your TypeScript project.

CI/CD pipelines automate tasks such as building, testing, and deploying your code.

Popular CI/CD platforms like Travis CI, CircleCI, or GitHub Actions can integrate with your TypeScript project and execute these tasks automatically whenever changes are pushed to your repository.

For example, you can set up a GitHub Actions workflow that runs your tests on every pull request and deploys your application to a staging environment when changes are merged into the main branch.

This automated process helps maintain code quality and ensures that your project remains scalable and reliable.

Furthermore, documenting your TypeScript code is essential for scalability.

Documentation provides clear guidance on how to use your code, making it easier for other developers (including your future self) to understand and work with it.

You can document your TypeScript code using comments, and TypeScript-specific tools like TypeDoc can generate documentation from your codebase.

Consider adding JSDoc comments to your functions and classes, providing descriptions, parameter explanations, and return value details:

typescriptCopy code

```
/** * Adds two numbers. * @param {number} a - The first number to add. * @param {number} b - The second number to add. * @returns {number} The sum of the two numbers. */ function add(a: number, b: number): number { return a + b; }
```

With proper documentation, you empower other developers to use your code effectively, reducing the learning curve and enhancing your project's scalability.

Version control is another critical aspect of managing a scalable TypeScript project.

Using a version control system (VCS) like Git enables you to track changes, collaborate with others, and roll back to previous states if issues arise.

When working on a TypeScript project, consider following best practices for Git usage, such as using meaningful commit messages, branching strategies (e.g., feature branches, release branches), and utilizing pull requests or merge requests for code reviews.

Effective version control ensures that your project remains organized, collaborative, and adaptable to changes.

As your TypeScript project grows, you may find it beneficial to leverage package management tools like npm or Yarn to manage dependencies.

These tools simplify the process of installing, updating, and sharing libraries and packages.

When adding dependencies to your project, ensure that you document them in a "package.json" file and specify their versions to maintain consistency and prevent unexpected breaking changes.

Additionally, consider implementing a dependency update strategy, regularly reviewing and updating packages to benefit from bug fixes, performance improvements, and security patches.

TypeScript's support for type definitions for packages, available through DefinitelyTyped, enhances dependency management by providing type safety when using external libraries.

When working on large-scale TypeScript projects, you'll likely need to optimize your build and bundling process for performance and scalability.

Tools like Webpack and Parcel are commonly used to bundle TypeScript code and assets for production.

Webpack, for example, allows you to define entry points, configure loaders for TypeScript, and generate optimized bundles.

To set up Webpack for a TypeScript project, you can install the necessary dependencies:

bashCopy code

```
npm install webpack webpack-cli webpack-dev-server
--save-dev npm install ts-loader typescript --save-dev
```

Next, create a "webpack.config.js" file to configure Webpack:

javascriptCopy code

```
const path = require('path'); module.exports = {
entry: './src/index.ts', output: { filename:
'bundle.js', path: path.resolve(__dirname, 'dist'), },
module: { rules: [ { test: /\.tsx?$/, use: 'ts-loader',
exclude: /node_modules/, }, ], }, resolve: {
extensions: ['.tsx', '.ts', '.js'], }, };
```

This configuration defines an entry point, output file, and loader for TypeScript files.

By optimizing your build process with bundlers like Webpack, you can reduce load times and ensure that your TypeScript project remains performant as it scales.

In summary, building scalable TypeScript projects requires a combination of effective code organization, proper type annotations, automated testing, documentation, version control, dependency management, and optimized build processes.

By following best practices and adopting these strategies, you can create TypeScript projects that can evolve, grow, and remain maintainable as they scale in complexity and size.

Next, we will delve into real-world project examples and case studies to showcase how TypeScript can be applied effectively in various scenarios.

Let's begin with an exploration of TypeScript's role in frontend web development.

Frontend Development: Frontend web development involves building user interfaces (UIs) and user experiences (UXs) for websites and web applications. TypeScript has gained significant popularity in this domain, particularly when working with modern frontend libraries and frameworks like React, Angular, and Vue.js.

For instance, in a real-world React project, TypeScript can be used to create type-safe components and manage complex state structures. To start a new React project with TypeScript, you can use the Create React App tool with the TypeScript template:

bashCopy code

```
npx create-react-app my-ts-app --template typescript
```

This command sets up a new React project with TypeScript, providing type safety and better code organization. TypeScript's type checking helps prevent common errors in large-scale React applications.

In an Angular application, TypeScript is the primary language for building components, services, and modules. The Angular CLI, a powerful command-line tool for Angular development, supports TypeScript out of the box. To create a new Angular project with TypeScript, you can use the following command:
bashCopy code

```
ng new my-ng-app
```

TypeScript enhances the development experience in Angular by enabling features like type checking, code navigation, and refactoring support.

Similarly, Vue.js developers can benefit from TypeScript's static typing when building Vue components. To set up a new Vue project with TypeScript support, you can use the Vue CLI:
bashCopy code

```
vue create my-vue-app
```

TypeScript seamlessly integrates with Vue.js, providing type safety for props, data, and methods within components.

Backend Development: TypeScript isn't limited to frontend development—it's also a valuable tool for building robust backend applications. Node.js, a popular runtime for server-side JavaScript, works seamlessly with TypeScript.

For instance, consider a real-world Node.js project using the Express.js framework. To start a new Express.js project with TypeScript, you can follow these steps:

Initialize a Node.js project:

bashCopy code

npm init -y

Install TypeScript and Express.js:

bashCopy code

npm install typescript express @types/express --save

Create a TypeScript configuration file (tsconfig.json):

bashCopy code

npx tsc --init

Modify the tsconfig.json file to specify the "outDir" as "dist" for compiled files.

Create a server.ts file and set up your Express.js application.

Write your server logic, routes, and middleware using TypeScript.

Compile the TypeScript code to JavaScript:

bashCopy code

npx tsc

Start the Express.js server:

bashCopy code

node dist/server.js

This setup allows you to build scalable and maintainable backend APIs with the benefits of TypeScript's static typing.

TypeScript's role in backend development extends beyond Express.js. It can be used with various Node.js frameworks and libraries, enabling developers to create type-safe server applications.

Mobile App Development: TypeScript is not limited to web development; it is also a valuable choice for mobile app development. When building mobile apps with technologies like React Native or NativeScript, TypeScript enhances the development process.

For instance, React Native allows you to develop mobile apps for both iOS and Android using React and JavaScript. However, you can use TypeScript to bring type safety to your React Native projects. To create a new React Native project with TypeScript, you can use the following command:

bashCopy code

```
npx react-native init MyRNApp --template react-native-template-typescript
```

This sets up a React Native project with TypeScript support, allowing you to write type-safe code for your mobile app.

Similarly, NativeScript, a framework for building native mobile apps using web technologies, supports TypeScript. You can create a new NativeScript project with TypeScript by running:

bashCopy code

```
tns create MyNSApp --template tns-template-blank-ng-ts
```

TypeScript's static typing enhances the development experience in mobile app projects, reducing runtime errors and improving code quality.

Cross-Platform Desktop Apps: TypeScript is not limited to web and mobile development; it can also be used to build cross-platform desktop applications.

Electron, a framework for creating desktop apps using web technologies, fully supports TypeScript.

To start a new Electron project with TypeScript, you can use the Electron Forge command-line tool:

bashCopy code

```
npx create-electron-app my-electron-app --template=typescript
```

This command sets up a new Electron project with TypeScript support, allowing you to build desktop applications with the benefits of type safety and modern web development techniques.

In summary, TypeScript is a versatile language that can be applied effectively across various domains, including frontend and backend web development, mobile app development, and cross-platform desktop app development. Real-world projects and case studies demonstrate how TypeScript enhances the development experience, improves code quality, and ensures maintainability in a wide range of application scenarios.

BOOK 3
TYPESCRIPT IN DEPTH
BUILDING WEB APPLICATIONS: EXPLORING
TYPESCRIPT WITH REAL-WORLD WEB DEVELOPMENT
PROJECTS

ROB BOTWRIGHT

Chapter 1: Introduction to Web Development with TypeScript

In the rapidly evolving landscape of web development, TypeScript has emerged as a powerful and versatile tool that plays a significant role in modern web development practices. TypeScript, often abbreviated as TS, is a statically typed superset of JavaScript, and it brings numerous advantages to the web development process.

Web development has come a long way since the early days of static HTML pages. Today, web applications are complex, dynamic, and interactive, and they require robust tools and technologies to meet the demands of users and businesses. TypeScript addresses many of the challenges faced by modern web developers.

One of the primary advantages of TypeScript is its static type system. Unlike JavaScript, where variables can change types at runtime, TypeScript enforces type constraints at compile-time. This means that you can catch type-related errors before your code ever runs, leading to more robust and predictable web applications.

To illustrate the significance of TypeScript's static typing, consider a scenario where you're developing a web application that calculates and displays the total price of items in a shopping cart. With TypeScript, you can define precise types for your data structures, such as the item object and the shopping cart array.

For instance, you can define an interface for the item object:

typescriptCopy code

interface Item { id: number; name: string; price: number; }

You can also define a type for the shopping cart:

typescriptCopy code

type ShoppingCart = Item[];

With these type definitions in place, TypeScript ensures that you only work with items and shopping carts that adhere to the specified structure. If you attempt to assign an object that doesn't match the Item interface or a variable that doesn't conform to the ShoppingCart type, TypeScript will raise a compilation error.

This static type checking is invaluable for catching potential bugs early in the development process, reducing the likelihood of runtime errors that can lead to unexpected behavior in your web application.

In addition to enhancing the reliability of your code, TypeScript provides improved code readability and maintainability. By explicitly defining types and interfaces, you make your code self-documenting, enabling both you and other developers to understand the data structures and function signatures without extensive comments or documentation.

TypeScript also encourages the use of modern JavaScript features and syntax, making it a natural fit for contemporary web development. You can leverage features like arrow functions, destructuring, async/await, and class-based components in web applications developed with TypeScript.

For example, if you're using React, a popular JavaScript library for building user interfaces, TypeScript offers excellent support. You can create type-safe React components by defining PropTypes or using TypeScript's native type annotations.

Here's an example of a simple React component with TypeScript:

typescriptCopy code

```
import React, { FC } from 'react'; interface GreetingProps { name: string; } const Greeting: FC<GreetingProps> = ({ name }) => { return <div>Hello, {name}!</div>; }; export default Greeting;
```

In this code, the Greeting component accepts a prop named "name" of type string. TypeScript ensures that you only pass valid props to this component, and it offers auto-completion and type checking in modern code editors.

TypeScript also shines when working with asynchronous operations. When making API calls or handling asynchronous events, TypeScript's support for async/await simplifies the code and ensures that promises and asynchronous functions are used correctly.

For instance, consider a scenario where you need to fetch data from an API using the Fetch API in a React component:

typescriptCopy code

```typescript
import React, { FC, useEffect, useState } from 'react';
interface Post { userId: number; id: number; title: string; body: string; } const Posts: FC = () => { const [posts, setPosts] = useState<Post[]>([]); useEffect(() => { const fetchData = async () => { try { const response = await fetch('https://jsonplaceholder.typicode.com/posts'); if (!response.ok) { throw new Error('Network response was not ok'); } const data = await response.json(); setPosts(data); } catch (error) { console.error('Error fetching data:', error); } }; fetchData(); }, []); return ( <ul> {posts.map((post) => ( <li key={post.id}>{post.title}</li> ))} </ul> ); }; export default Posts;
```

In this React component, TypeScript ensures that you handle potential errors properly, and it provides type annotations for the fetched data, making it clear what data structure to expect.

Furthermore, TypeScript's tooling support is extensive, with robust integrations into popular code editors like Visual Studio Code, enabling features like auto-completion, type inference, and real-time error checking.

The TypeScript compiler (tsc) provides powerful options for customizing compilation behavior and targeting different ECMAScript versions, ensuring compatibility with a wide range of browsers and environments.

Additionally, TypeScript's rich ecosystem includes declaration files for many popular libraries and frameworks. These declaration files, often found on DefinitelyTyped, provide type definitions for third-party JavaScript libraries, enabling you to use them seamlessly in your TypeScript projects while preserving type safety.

TypeScript also facilitates collaboration in web development teams. With well-defined type annotations and interfaces, team members can understand and interact with the codebase more effectively. Code reviews become smoother, and the likelihood of introducing subtle bugs through code changes is reduced.

When it comes to testing web applications, TypeScript's type system aids in writing comprehensive test suites. Testing libraries like Jest and Testing Library offer TypeScript support, ensuring that your tests are type-safe and accurately reflect the behavior of your code.

Deploying web applications developed with TypeScript follows the same principles as deploying traditional JavaScript applications. You bundle and optimize your code for production, configure hosting and server settings, and follow best practices for performance, security, and scalability.

In summary, TypeScript has become an integral part of modern web development. Its static type system, code readability, and maintainability benefits, along with its support for contemporary JavaScript features, make it a valuable tool for building robust and reliable web applications. Whether you're working on frontend, backend, or cross-platform development, TypeScript enhances your development experience and contributes to the success of your web projects.

Chapter 2: Setting Up a TypeScript Web Development Environment

Selecting the right development tools is a crucial decision that significantly influences the success of a software project.

In the ever-evolving landscape of software development, a wide range of tools, frameworks, and technologies are available, each catering to specific needs and preferences.

Before diving into the various tools available, it's essential to have a clear understanding of your project's requirements, goals, and constraints.

Start by defining the scope of your project, including the type of application you're building, its intended audience, and its technical specifications.

Consider the programming languages you're familiar with and the ones best suited for the project.

Once you've defined your project's requirements, you can begin evaluating and selecting the development tools that align with your objectives.

One of the fundamental decisions is choosing a code editor or integrated development environment (IDE).

Code editors like Visual Studio Code, Sublime Text, and Atom offer lightweight and customizable environments that are well-suited for a wide range of programming languages, including TypeScript.

They provide features like syntax highlighting, code completion, and extensions that can enhance your TypeScript development experience.

On the other hand, IDEs like Visual Studio, WebStorm, and IntelliJ IDEA offer comprehensive environments specifically designed for software development.

They provide advanced features such as integrated debugging, refactoring tools, and powerful TypeScript support.

Your choice between a code editor and an IDE depends on your familiarity with the tool, your workflow preferences, and the complexity of your project.

Once you've selected a code editor or IDE, it's essential to configure it for TypeScript development.

Most modern editors and IDEs offer TypeScript plugins or extensions that simplify the setup process.

For example, in Visual Studio Code, you can install the "TypeScript" extension from the Visual Studio Code Marketplace.

This extension provides TypeScript language support, type checking, and TypeScript-specific features.

Additionally, you can configure your TypeScript project settings by creating a "tsconfig.json" file in your project directory.

This configuration file allows you to specify TypeScript compiler options, target ECMAScript versions, and other project-specific settings.

When working on a TypeScript project, it's essential to maintain consistent code style and formatting.

You can achieve this by using code formatting tools like Prettier or ESLint with TypeScript plugins.

Prettier is an opinionated code formatter that enforces consistent code style by automatically formatting your code to adhere to predefined rules.

To use Prettier with TypeScript, you can install the "prettier" package and configure it in your project's ".prettierrc" or ".prettier.config.js" file.

For ESLint, a popular linting tool, you can use the "eslint-plugin-typescript" plugin to enforce TypeScript-specific rules and conventions.

To get started with ESLint and TypeScript, you can follow the official ESLint documentation.

Version control is another critical aspect of software development.

Git, a distributed version control system, is widely adopted in the development community.

Using Git allows you to track changes, collaborate with team members, and manage your codebase effectively.

To initialize a Git repository for your TypeScript project, navigate to your project directory in the command line and run the following command:

csharpCopy code

```
git init
```

This command initializes a new Git repository, and you can start committing your code changes.

Additionally, hosting platforms like GitHub, GitLab, and Bitbucket offer online repositories for storing and collaborating on your Git projects.

By creating a remote repository on one of these platforms, you can easily push your code changes, collaborate with team members, and keep your project's history in a secure and accessible location.

Another consideration when choosing development tools is the build and deployment process.

TypeScript code must be transpiled to JavaScript before it can run in a browser or Node.js environment.

For this purpose, TypeScript provides a compiler called "tsc" that converts TypeScript code into JavaScript.

To install TypeScript globally and use the "tsc" compiler, you can run the following command:

Copy code

```
npm install -g typescript
```

After installing TypeScript, you can transpile your TypeScript files by running the "tsc" command followed by the name of your TypeScript file:

Copy code

```
tsc myFile.ts
```

This command generates a corresponding JavaScript file, such as "myFile.js," in the same directory.

However, managing TypeScript compilation manually can become cumbersome in larger projects.

To streamline the build process, you can use build tools like Webpack or Parcel.

These tools automate tasks such as bundling, minification, and code splitting, making your development workflow more efficient.

Webpack, in particular, is a popular choice for TypeScript projects.

To set up Webpack for a TypeScript project, you can create a "webpack.config.js" file in your project directory and configure the entry point, output file, and TypeScript loader.

Additionally, you can use plugins like "ts-loader" or "awesome-typescript-loader" to seamlessly integrate TypeScript with Webpack.

Once your TypeScript project is built and ready for deployment, you'll need to consider the hosting environment.

The choice of hosting platform depends on the type of application you're building.

For web applications, platforms like Netlify, Vercel, and AWS Amplify offer simple and scalable hosting solutions.

You can deploy your TypeScript application to one of these platforms by connecting your Git repository and specifying your build and deployment settings.

For server-side applications, platforms like Heroku, AWS Lambda, and Google Cloud Functions provide serverless deployment options.

These platforms allow you to deploy TypeScript-based serverless functions and APIs without managing server infrastructure.

In summary, choosing the right development tools is a critical decision that can significantly impact the success of your TypeScript project.

Start by defining your project's requirements and objectives, and then select the code editor or IDE that aligns with your workflow and preferences.

Configure your development environment for TypeScript by installing the necessary extensions and plugins, and create a "tsconfig.json" file to manage TypeScript compiler settings.

Maintain consistent code style and formatting using tools like Prettier and ESLint, and ensure proper version control with Git and online repositories.

Streamline the build process by using build tools like Webpack or Parcel, and consider the hosting platform that best suits your application's needs.

By carefully choosing and configuring your development tools, you can create a productive and efficient development environment for your TypeScript projects.

Chapter 3: Building a Simple TypeScript Web Page

To embark on the journey of web development, you must first create a solid foundation, and that starts with crafting a basic HTML structure.

HTML, or Hypertext Markup Language, is the backbone of the web, serving as the structure upon which all web content is built.

It is essential to understand how to create a well-structured HTML document to ensure your web pages are accessible, readable, and maintainable.

Begin by opening your preferred code editor or integrated development environment (IDE).

Popular choices for code editors include Visual Studio Code, Sublime Text, Atom, and many others, all of which provide a comfortable environment for writing HTML code.

In your code editor, create a new file and save it with an ".html" extension, such as "index.html," to indicate that it is an HTML document.

Before delving into the details of the HTML structure, it's helpful to understand the basic anatomy of an HTML document.

An HTML document consists of elements, which are the building blocks of a web page.

Each element is enclosed within opening and closing tags, and together they define the element's content and purpose.

The most fundamental element in an HTML document is the **<!DOCTYPE html>** declaration, which specifies the document type and version.

This declaration should always be the first line of your HTML document, ensuring that the browser knows to interpret the content as HTML5.

Following the **<!DOCTYPE html>** declaration, you will have an opening **<html>** tag, which encloses the entire HTML document.

Within the **<html>** tag, you will typically find two main sections: the **<head>** and the **<body>**.

The **<head>** section contains metadata about the document, such as the title, character set, and links to external resources like stylesheets and scripts.

The **<body>** section, on the other hand, contains the visible content of the web page, including text, images, links, and other elements that users interact with.

To create a basic HTML structure, start by opening your document with the **<!DOCTYPE html>** declaration:

htmlCopy code

<!DOCTYPE html>

Followed by the **<html>** element:

htmlCopy code

<!DOCTYPE html> <html> </html>

Inside the **<html>** element, you will place the **<head>** and **<body>** sections.

The **<head>** section typically includes a **<meta>** tag to specify the character encoding, ensuring that special characters and symbols display correctly in the browser.

Here's an example of a minimal **<head>** section:

htmlCopy code

```
<!DOCTYPE html> <html> <head> <meta
charset="UTF-8"> <title>My First Web Page</title>
</head> </html>
```

In this example, the **<meta>** tag specifies the character encoding as UTF-8, which is a widely used character set that supports a broad range of characters and symbols.

The **<title>** element sets the title of the web page, which appears in the browser's title bar or tab.

With the **<head>** section in place, you can move on to the **<body>** section, where you will add the visible content of your web page.

Inside the **<body>** element, you can include various HTML elements to structure your content.

For instance, you can use headings (**<h1>**, **<h2>**, **<h3>**, etc.) to define the main headings and subheadings of your page:

htmlCopy code

```
<!DOCTYPE html> <html> <head> <meta
charset="UTF-8"> <title>My First Web Page</title>
</head> <body> <h1>Welcome to My Web
Page</h1> <p>This is a paragraph of text.</p>
<h2>About Me</h2> <p>I'm a web developer with a
passion for coding.</p> </body> </html>
```

In this example, the **<h1>** element represents the main heading of the page, while the **<h2>** element is used for a subsection.

Paragraphs of text are enclosed within **<p>** elements, providing a logical and semantic structure to the content.

HTML also allows you to add links to other web pages using the **<a>** (anchor) element:

htmlCopy code

```
<a            href="https://www.example.com">Visit
Example.com</a>
```

This code creates a link that, when clicked, takes the user to the specified URL.

Images can be included in your web page using the **<img>** element, with the **src** attribute pointing to the image file:

htmlCopy code

```
<img src="image.jpg" alt="An example image">
```

In this code, the **src** attribute specifies the path to the image file, while the **alt** attribute provides alternative text that is displayed if the image cannot be loaded or for accessibility purposes.

Lists are another essential element in HTML, and you can create both ordered (numbered) and unordered (bulleted) lists using the **<ol>** and **<ul>** elements, respectively:

htmlCopy code

<ol> <li>Item 1</li> <li>Item 2</li> <li>Item 3</li> </ol> <ul> <li>First item</li> <li>Second item</li> <li>Third item</li> </ul>

These are just a few of the many HTML elements you can use to structure and format your web page content.

Additionally, HTML provides attributes that allow you to further customize and enhance elements.

For example, you can add the **class** attribute to elements to apply CSS styles, and the **id** attribute to create unique identifiers for specific elements.

htmlCopy code

<p class="important-text">This text has a special style.</p> <div id="unique-section">This section has a unique identifier.</div>

To preview your web page in a browser, you can simply open the HTML file in your preferred browser.

However, for more comprehensive development and testing, you may consider setting up a local development server.

Popular choices for local development servers include Node.js with the **http-server** package or Python's built-in **http.server** module.

To set up a simple Node.js server, you can use the following commands:

bashCopy code

Install the http-server package globally (if not already installed) npm install -g http-server # Navigate to your project directory cd

/path/to/your/project # Start the local development server http-server

This will start a server on a specific port (usually 8080) and provide a local URL (e.g., http://localhost:8080) where you can access your web page during development.

In summary, creating a basic HTML structure is the first step in web development, and it forms the foundation upon which you build your web pages.

Understanding the fundamental structure of an HTML document, including the **\<head\>** and **\<body\>** sections, is essential.

By using HTML elements and attributes, you can structure and format your content effectively, and with the help of a local development server, you can preview and test your web pages locally before deploying them to the web.

Chapter 4: Managing State and Data in Web Applications

Data handling and storage are critical aspects of software development, as they determine how information is collected, processed, and preserved.

In modern applications, data comes in various forms, such as text, numbers, images, and more, and effective data management is essential for creating functional and efficient software.

One of the fundamental techniques for data handling is data input and output, where information is gathered from users and presented to them.

In command-line applications, the process often involves reading input from the user and displaying output on the terminal.

To read user input in a command-line environment, you can use standard input (stdin) and functions like **readline** in Node.js or input streams in other programming languages.

For instance, in Node.js, you can collect user input with the following code:

javascriptCopy code

```
const readline = require('readline'); const rl =
readline.createInterface({ input: process.stdin,
output: process.stdout }); rl.question('What is your
```

name? ', (name) => { console.log(`Hello, ${name}!`); rl.close(); });

In this example, the **readline** module is used to prompt the user for their name and then display a greeting message.

Once you have gathered and processed data, you may need to store it for future use or analysis.

Data storage techniques vary depending on the type and volume of data, as well as the requirements of your application.

One common method is to use flat files, such as text or CSV files, to store structured data.

To write data to a text file in a command-line application, you can use file I/O operations.

For example, in Node.js, you can write data to a file like this:

javascriptCopy code

```
const fs = require('fs'); const data = 'This is some data to write to a file.'; fs.writeFileSync('data.txt', data);
```

This code snippet creates a file named "data.txt" and writes the specified data into it.

To read data from a file, you can use similar file I/O operations:

javascriptCopy code

```
const fs = require('fs'); const data = fs.readFileSync('data.txt', 'utf8'); console.log(data);
```

Here, the **readFileSync** function is used to read the contents of "data.txt" and then display them.

While flat files are suitable for simple data storage, databases are a more powerful and organized way to manage structured data.

Relational databases like MySQL, PostgreSQL, and SQLite offer structured storage and efficient querying capabilities.

To interact with a database from a command-line application, you can use database-specific command-line clients or libraries.

For example, if you are using PostgreSQL, you can connect to the database and execute SQL queries using the **psql** command:

bashCopy code

```
psql -U your_username -d your_database
```

Once connected, you can interact with the database by running SQL commands.

Another popular database option is SQLite, which is a lightweight, serverless database engine.

You can use the **sqlite3** command-line client to work with SQLite databases:

bashCopy code

```
sqlite3 your_database.db
```

This opens the SQLite shell, where you can execute SQL statements to manipulate data.

In addition to relational databases, NoSQL databases like MongoDB and Redis are suitable for handling unstructured or semi-structured data.

These databases often have command-line clients or libraries that allow you to interact with them from the command line.

For example, to connect to a MongoDB database using the **mongo** shell, you can run:

bashCopy code

```
mongo --host your_host_name --username your_username --password your_password your_database
```

This command opens the MongoDB shell, where you can perform operations on your data.

Beyond traditional databases, cloud-based storage solutions have gained popularity for their scalability and ease of use.

Services like Amazon S3, Google Cloud Storage, and Azure Blob Storage provide command-line tools that allow you to upload, download, and manage files and data in the cloud.

For instance, to upload a file to an Amazon S3 bucket using the AWS Command Line Interface (CLI), you can use the following command:

bashCopy code

```
aws s3 cp my_file.txt s3://your-bucket-name/
```

This command uploads "my_file.txt" to the specified S3 bucket.

To retrieve the file, you can use the **aws s3 cp** command with the opposite direction:

bashCopy code

```
aws s3 cp s3://your-bucket-name/my_file.txt .
```

This retrieves "my_file.txt" from the S3 bucket and stores it locally.

While data storage is a crucial part of data handling, data manipulation and transformation are equally essential.

In command-line applications, you can use various command-line tools and scripting languages to process data efficiently.

One powerful tool for data manipulation is the Unix shell, which provides commands like **grep**, **sed**, **awk**, and **sort** to filter, search, and transform data from the command line.

For example, you can use **grep** to search for specific lines in a text file that match a pattern:

bashCopy code

```
grep "error" log.txt
```

This command displays all lines in "log.txt" containing the word "error."

Similarly, **sed** and **awk** can be used to perform text replacements and text processing, respectively.

Another useful command is **sort**, which can sort lines in a file based on various criteria:

bashCopy code

```
sort -r data.txt
```

This command sorts the lines in "data.txt" in reverse order.

When dealing with structured data, scripting languages like Python, Ruby, and JavaScript can be powerful allies.

These languages offer libraries and modules for data manipulation, making it easier to perform complex operations.

For example, in Python, you can use the built-in **csv** module to read and write CSV files, which are commonly used for tabular data:

pythonCopy code

```
import csv # Reading a CSV file with open('data.csv', 'r') as csvfile: reader = csv.reader(csvfile) for row in reader: print(row) # Writing to a CSV file with open('output.csv', 'w') as csvfile: writer = csv.writer(csvfile) writer.writerow(['Name', 'Age']) writer.writerow(['Alice', 25]) writer.writerow(['Bob', 30])
```

In this Python code, the **csv** module is used to read data from "data.csv" and write data to "output.csv."

JavaScript, with libraries like **csv-parser** and **fast-csv**, can also handle CSV files efficiently.

Data validation and error handling are crucial aspects of data handling, ensuring that the data you work with is accurate and reliable.

In command-line applications, you can implement validation and error handling by incorporating conditional statements and error-checking mechanisms in your scripts.

For instance, you can use conditional statements to check if user-provided data meets specific criteria before processing it:

bashCopy code

```
read -p "Enter your age: " age if [[ $age -ge 18 ]];
then echo "You are eligible for this service." else
echo "Sorry, you are not eligible." fi
```

In this Bash script, the user's age is collected, and a conditional statement checks if it is greater than or equal to 18 to determine eligibility.

Additionally, you can implement error handling by using conditional constructs and exit codes to gracefully handle errors and exceptions.

For instance, in a Bash script, you can use the **exit** command to terminate the script with a specific exit code when an error occurs:

bashCopy code

```
if [ ! -f "file.txt" ]; then echo "File not found." exit 1
fi
```

Here, if the file "file.txt" does not exist, the script will exit with an exit code of 1, indicating an error.

When it comes to data storage techniques, data backups and version control play crucial roles in safeguarding your data and ensuring its integrity.

Regularly backing up your data to an external location or cloud storage is essential to prevent data loss in case of hardware failures or unforeseen incidents.

For local data backup, you can use tools like **rsync** on Unix-based systems to synchronize data between directories or devices.

To create a backup of a directory, you can run a command like this:

bashCopy code

rsync -av /source/directory/ /backup/directory/

This command copies all files and directories from the source directory to the backup directory.

For version control, Git is a widely adopted tool that allows you to track changes to your code and data over time.

Using Git, you can maintain a history of changes, collaborate with others, and easily revert to previous versions when needed.

To initialize a Git repository for your project, navigate to your project directory and run the following commands:

bashCopy code

```
git init git add . git commit -m "Initial commit"
```

This creates a Git repository, stages all files for the initial commit, and commits them with a descriptive message.

Subsequently, you can use Git to track changes, create branches for different features or versions, and collaborate with others by pushing and pulling changes from remote repositories.

Data handling and storage techniques are central to software development, ensuring that data is collected, processed, and preserved effectively.

Whether you are working with user input, files, databases, or cloud storage, understanding these techniques is essential for building robust and reliable applications.

Moreover, incorporating data validation, error handling, backups, and version control practices into your development process is crucial for maintaining data integrity and minimizing risks.

By mastering these techniques, you can navigate the complexities of data handling and storage in the world of software development.

Chapter 5: Interactivity and User Experience with TypeScript

In the ever-evolving landscape of web development, interactivity plays a central role in enhancing the user experience.

Interactivity is the key to engaging and captivating users, making them active participants rather than passive observers of a website or application.

As technology advances, users have come to expect dynamic and responsive interfaces that not only deliver information but also allow them to interact with the content.

One of the foundational technologies for creating interactive web pages and applications is JavaScript, a versatile and powerful programming language that runs in the browser.

JavaScript enables developers to add interactivity by responding to user actions, such as clicks, input, and gestures.

To harness the capabilities of JavaScript, you'll need to include it in your web pages.

This can be done by adding a **<script>** tag in the HTML document, either within the **<head>** section or just before the closing **</body>** tag.

Here's an example of how to include an external JavaScript file in your HTML:

htmlCopy code

```
<!DOCTYPE html> <html> <head> <title>Interactive
Web Page</title> </head> <body> <h1>Welcome
to the Interactive Web Page</h1> <button id="click-
me">Click              Me</button>              <script
src="script.js"></script> </body> </html>
```

In this example, the **<script>** tag references an
external JavaScript file named "script.js."

Inside "script.js," you can write JavaScript code to add
interactivity to your web page.

For instance, you can use JavaScript to respond to a
button click event and change the content of the page
dynamically:

javascriptCopy code

```
// script.js const button =
document.getElementById('click-me');
button.addEventListener('click', () => { const
heading = document.querySelector('h1');
heading.textContent = 'You clicked the button!'; });
```

In this code, JavaScript listens for a click event on the
button element with the id "click-me" and updates
the heading's text when the button is clicked.

This simple example demonstrates how JavaScript can
transform static web content into an interactive and
dynamic experience.

Beyond basic interactivity, JavaScript libraries and
frameworks, such as jQuery, React, Angular, and
Vue.js, provide tools and components that simplify
the development of complex and feature-rich web
applications.

For example, jQuery offers a concise and intuitive way to manipulate the DOM (Document Object Model), handle events, and perform AJAX requests.

Here's how you can use jQuery to toggle the visibility of an element:

javascriptCopy code

```
// Include jQuery in your HTML <script src="https://code.jquery.com/jquery-3.6.0.min.js"></script> // JavaScript code using jQuery $(document).ready(function() { $('#toggle-button').click(function() { $('#toggle-me').toggle(); }); });
```

In this snippet, clicking the button with the id "toggle-button" toggles the visibility of the element with the id "toggle-me."

React, on the other hand, is a component-based library for building user interfaces, enabling developers to create reusable UI elements and efficiently manage state and data flow.

Here's an example of a simple React component that counts button clicks:

javascriptCopy code

```
// Import React and ReactDOM in your HTML <script src="https://unpkg.com/react@17/umd/react.development.js"></script> <script src="https://unpkg.com/react-dom@17/umd/react-dom.development.js"></script> // JavaScript code using React class ClickCounter extends
```

```
React.Component { constructor(props) {
super(props); this.state = { count: 0 }; }
handleClick() { this.setState({ count:
this.state.count + 1 }); } render() { return ( <div>
<button onClick={() => this.handleClick()}>Click
me</button> <p>Clicked {this.state.count} times.</p>
</div> ); } } ReactDOM.render(<ClickCounter />,
document.getElementById('root'));
```

In this example, React manages the component's state and renders the UI dynamically based on the state changes.

The button click updates the count, and React re-renders the component to reflect the updated count value.

Adding interactivity to your web pages isn't limited to JavaScript libraries and frameworks; HTML5 and CSS3 offer native features for creating interactive elements.

For instance, HTML5 introduced the **<canvas>** element, which allows you to draw graphics and animations directly in the browser using JavaScript.

You can create dynamic visualizations, games, and interactive charts by manipulating the canvas with JavaScript.

Additionally, HTML5 brought native support for audio and video playback, enabling you to embed multimedia content in your web pages without the need for third-party plugins.

CSS3 introduced transitions and animations, allowing you to animate CSS properties smoothly.

You can create interactive hover effects, sliding panels, and other animations with CSS animations and transitions.

Here's a simple example of how to create a CSS transition for a button's background color on hover:

cssCopy code

```
/* Add CSS to your HTML file */ <style> .button {
background-color: #3498db; color: #fff; padding:
10px 20px; border: none; cursor: pointer;
transition: background-color 0.3s ease-in-out; }
.button:hover { background-color: #2980b9; }
</style>
```

In this CSS code, the **.button** class specifies a background color transition when the button is hovered over.

This provides a smooth color change effect that enhances the user experience.

Interactivity also extends to responsive design, ensuring that web applications and websites adapt seamlessly to various screen sizes and devices.

Responsive web design techniques, such as media queries and flexible layouts, allow you to create user-friendly experiences on both desktop and mobile devices.

For example, you can use media queries to apply different styles and layouts based on the screen width:

cssCopy code

```
/* Add CSS to your HTML file */ <style> /* Default
styles for desktop */ .container { width: 960px;
margin: 0 auto; } /* Media query for screens smaller
than 768px (e.g., mobile) */ @media (max-width:
768px) { .container { width: 100%; padding: 0
20px; } } </style>
```

In this CSS code, the **.container** class is styled differently for desktop and mobile screens using a media query.

For screens smaller than 768 pixels wide, the container becomes full-width and has reduced padding.

This ensures that content remains readable and accessible on various devices, enhancing the user experience.

Another aspect of interactivity in web development is user feedback and validation.

Providing immediate feedback to users when they interact with your application can improve user satisfaction and reduce errors.

You can achieve this through techniques like form validation, tooltips, and progress indicators.

For instance, form validation ensures that users provide valid input before submitting a form.

HTML5 introduced various input types and attributes that support client-side validation, such as "required," "email," and "pattern."

Here's an example of an HTML form with client-side validation:

htmlCopy code

```
<form> <label for="email">Email:</label> <input type="email" id="email" name="email" required> <input type="submit" value="Submit"> </form>
```

In this form, the "email" input field is marked as "required" and uses the "email" input type, ensuring that users enter a valid email address before submitting the form.

Additionally, you can provide real-time feedback to users as they fill out a form by using JavaScript to validate input and display error messages or success messages dynamically.

Tooltips are another valuable tool for enhancing interactivity and user experience.

By adding tooltips to elements with additional information or explanations, you can provide context and guidance to users when they hover over or interact with those elements.

CSS and JavaScript can be used to create custom tooltips or leverage existing tooltip libraries for added convenience.

Progress indicators, such as loading spinners or progress bars, inform users about ongoing processes or delays in your application.

You can use CSS animations or JavaScript libraries to implement these indicators and keep users informed about the status of their interactions.

In summary, enhancing user experience with interactivity is a fundamental aspect of modern web development.

Whether you're using JavaScript, libraries, or native HTML and CSS features, interactivity empowers you to create engaging and responsive web applications.

By understanding the tools and techniques available, you can design user-friendly interfaces, provide immediate feedback, and ensure that your web pages adapt gracefully to different devices and screen sizes.

Interactivity is the key to keeping users engaged and satisfied with your web applications, ultimately contributing to their success in today's digital landscape.

Chapter 6: Form Handling and Validation

Validating user input is a critical aspect of software development, ensuring that the data your application receives is accurate and reliable.

When users interact with your application, they provide input through various forms and interfaces, such as text fields, checkboxes, and dropdowns.

However, not all user input is valid or conforms to the expected format, and errors or malicious data can compromise the functionality and security of your application.

Next, we'll explore the importance of validating user input, common validation techniques, and how to implement input validation using TypeScript.

Validation serves several essential purposes in your application, including data integrity, security, and user experience.

First and foremost, input validation ensures data integrity by preventing invalid or malformed data from entering your application.

Invalid data can disrupt the functionality of your software, leading to unexpected errors and bugs.

For example, if you expect a user to enter an email address but allow any arbitrary text, it can lead to issues when trying to send emails or perform other email-related operations.

Secondly, input validation plays a crucial role in security.

Unvalidated user input is a common attack vector for security vulnerabilities such as SQL injection and cross-site scripting (XSS).

By validating input, you can mitigate these risks and protect your application and its users from potential threats.

For instance, validating that user-submitted data doesn't contain malicious scripts or unauthorized SQL queries can prevent attackers from exploiting vulnerabilities.

Lastly, input validation contributes to a positive user experience.

When users provide input, they expect feedback and guidance.

Validating input and providing clear error messages or suggestions help users correct mistakes and interact with your application more effectively.

Imagine a scenario where a user is filling out a registration form, and they enter an invalid email address.

Without validation and proper feedback, they might submit the form and receive an error message only after waiting for the server's response.

This can be frustrating and time-consuming for users, potentially leading to abandonment of the registration process.

To address these concerns, input validation is typically implemented on both the client and server sides.

Client-side validation occurs within the user's browser and provides immediate feedback to users as they interact with your application's forms and interfaces.

Server-side validation, on the other hand, is performed on the server once the user submits the data.

Server-side validation is essential for security and data integrity, as client-side validation can be bypassed or manipulated by malicious users.

However, client-side validation offers a more responsive and user-friendly experience.

In TypeScript, you can leverage the language's strong typing and validation features to implement client-side validation effectively.

One common approach to client-side validation in TypeScript is using conditional statements and regular expressions to check the format and validity of user input.

For example, to validate an email address input field, you can create a function that checks if the entered text matches the expected email format:

```typescript
typescriptCopy code
function isValidEmail(email: string): boolean { const
emailRegex  =  /^[A-Za-z0-9._%+-]+@[A-Za-z0-9.-
]+\.[A-Z|a-z]{2,}$/; return emailRegex.test(email); }
```

In this code, the **isValidEmail** function uses a regular expression to validate the email format.

When a user submits a form with an email field, you can call this function to validate the email input.

If the input is not in the expected email format, you can display an error message to the user.

Similarly, you can implement validation functions for other types of input, such as phone numbers, dates, or passwords, using appropriate regular expressions and conditions.

Another approach to client-side validation in TypeScript is leveraging libraries and frameworks that provide pre-built validation rules and error handling.

Popular libraries like Formik, Yup, and VeeValidate offer tools and components that simplify the process of implementing validation in forms.

For instance, Formik, a form management library for React, provides a built-in validation mechanism that allows you to define validation rules for form fields.

Here's an example of how you can use Formik for client-side validation in a React component:

typescriptCopy code

```
import React from 'react'; import { Formik, Field,
Form, ErrorMessage } from 'formik'; function
SignupForm() { return ( <Formik initialValues={{
email: '', password: '' }} validate={(values) => { const
errors: { [key: string]: string } = {}; if (!values.email) {
errors.email = 'Email is required'; } else if
(!isValidEmail(values.email)) { errors.email = 'Invalid
email address'; } if (!values.password) {
errors.password = 'Password is required'; } return
errors; }} onSubmit={(values) => { // Handle form
submission }} > <Form> <div> <label
```

```
htmlFor="email">Email</label> <Field type="email"
name="email" /> <ErrorMessage name="email"
component="div" className="error" /> </div> <div>
<label htmlFor="password">Password</label> <Field
type="password"        name="password"        />
<ErrorMessage name="password" component="div"
className="error" /> </div> <div> <button
type="submit">Submit</button> </div> </Form>
</Formik> ); }
```

In this example, Formik provides a **validate** function
where you can define custom validation logic for each
form field.

The error messages are displayed using the
ErrorMessage component.

This approach simplifies the integration of validation
into your forms and ensures a consistent user
experience.

While client-side validation is essential for providing
immediate feedback and enhancing the user
experience, server-side validation remains the
ultimate authority on data integrity and security.

To implement server-side validation, you need to
handle user input on the server, validate it, and return
validation results to the client.

Here's a simplified example using Node.js and Express
to handle a POST request with form data and perform
server-side validation:

typescriptCopy code

```
import express from 'express'; const app =
express(); app.use(express.json());
app.post('/register', (req, res) => { const { email,
password } = req.body; const errors: { [key: string]:
string } = {}; if (!email) { errors.email = 'Email is
required'; } else if (!isValidEmail(email)) {
errors.email = 'Invalid email address'; } if
(!password) { errors.password = 'Password is
required'; } if (Object.keys(errors).length > 0) {
res.status(400).json({ errors }); } else { // Perform
registration logic res.status(200).json({ message:
'Registration successful' }); } }); app.listen(3000, () =>
{ console.log('Server is running on port 3000'); });
```

In this server-side code, an Express route handles
POST requests to the "/register" endpoint.

The server-side validation checks the email and
password fields for errors and responds with the
appropriate error messages if validation fails.

Server-side validation is crucial because it prevents
invalid data from reaching your application's logic and
ensures that the data is clean and safe to use.

When implementing user input validation, consider
the following best practices:

Always validate input on the server side to ensure
data integrity and security.

Provide clear and user-friendly error messages to
guide users in correcting input errors.

Use established libraries and frameworks for client-side validation to simplify implementation and ensure consistency.

Regularly update and review your validation rules to adapt to changing requirements and security concerns.

Consider implementing server-side rate limiting and security mechanisms to protect against abuse and attacks.

In summary, validating user input with TypeScript is a critical aspect of developing robust and secure applications.

By implementing both client-side and server-side validation, you can ensure data integrity, enhance security, and provide a positive user experience.

Utilize TypeScript's strong typing and validation features to create reliable validation logic, and consider leveraging libraries and frameworks to streamline the process.

With effective input validation, your application can handle user input with confidence, reducing errors and vulnerabilities.

Chapter 7: Routing and Navigation in TypeScript Apps

Navigating between pages in single-page applications (SPAs) is a fundamental aspect of web development that significantly impacts user experience and application flow.

Unlike traditional multi-page applications, where each page corresponds to a separate HTML file and a full page reload occurs when transitioning between pages, SPAs load a single HTML file and dynamically update the content as users navigate.

This approach allows for smoother and more responsive user interfaces, but it also requires careful handling of navigation to maintain a consistent user experience.

Next, we'll explore various techniques and best practices for navigating between pages in SPAs.

The primary goal of navigation in SPAs is to provide users with the illusion of moving between different pages while keeping the application's core structure intact.

This illusion is achieved by manipulating the URL and updating the content displayed to users as they interact with the application.

To begin, it's essential to understand how SPAs handle navigation and maintain their state.

In a traditional multi-page application, each page corresponds to a unique URL, and the browser handles navigation by requesting and rendering the appropriate HTML file when a user clicks on a link or enters a URL in the address bar.

In contrast, SPAs use client-side routing to manage navigation.

Client-side routing intercepts URL changes and uses JavaScript to determine which content to display based on the requested URL.

This means that when a user clicks on a link within an SPA, the application intercepts the navigation event and updates the content dynamically without triggering a full page reload.

To implement client-side routing, SPAs often rely on JavaScript libraries or frameworks designed for this purpose.

One popular library for client-side routing is React Router, which provides a declarative way to manage navigation in React applications.

Here's a simplified example of how React Router can be used to define routes and handle navigation within an SPA:

javascriptCopy code

```javascript
import React from 'react'; import { BrowserRouter as Router, Route, Link } from 'react-router-dom'; function Home() { return <h1>Welcome to the Home Page!</h1>; } function About() { return <h1>Learn more about us on the About Page.</h1>; }
```

```
function App() { return ( <Router> <nav> <ul> <li>
<Link to="/">Home</Link> </li> <li> <Link
to="/about">About</Link> </li> </ul> </nav> <Route
path="/" exact component={Home} /> <Route
path="/about" component={About} /> </Router> ); }
export default App;
```

In this example, React Router is used to define two routes: one for the home page ("/") and another for the about page ("/about").

When users click on the provided links, React Router handles the navigation, rendering the corresponding components without a full page reload.

This client-side routing approach ensures a seamless user experience and allows developers to build SPAs with multiple "pages."

In addition to libraries like React Router, other JavaScript frameworks, such as Angular and Vue.js, offer their routing solutions for SPAs.

Regardless of the specific library or framework used, the key principles of navigation in SPAs remain consistent.

One significant advantage of client-side routing in SPAs is the ability to update the URL dynamically as users navigate.

This feature provides several benefits, such as the ability to share specific application states via URLs, enabling users to bookmark pages, and supporting the browser's forward and backward navigation buttons.

To update the URL dynamically, SPAs use a JavaScript method called **pushState** or **replaceState** from the History API.

Here's an example of how to use **pushState** to update the URL without triggering a full page reload:

javascriptCopy code

```
// Change the URL to '/about' history.pushState(null, null, '/about');
```

In this code, **history.pushState** changes the URL to "/about" without making an actual HTTP request to the server.

This allows the SPA to update its content based on the new URL, providing users with the impression of navigating to a different page.

It's important to note that while client-side routing and URL manipulation offer advantages, they also introduce challenges.

For example, when users refresh the page or enter a URL manually, the browser sends a request to the server for the specified URL.

Since SPAs typically load a single HTML file, the server may return a 404 error if the requested URL does not correspond to a valid server-side route.

To address this issue, server configurations and routing rules must be set up to ensure that the SPA is loaded for all routes and that the SPA can correctly interpret the requested URL on the client side.

This configuration may involve using a server-side technology like Node.js or configuring server rules for platforms like Apache or Nginx.

Server-side routing ensures that even when users enter a URL directly or refresh the page, the SPA can handle the request and display the appropriate content.

Another consideration in SPAs is managing application state across different pages.

In traditional multi-page applications, each page can have its own state, which is reset when the user navigates to another page.

In SPAs, the application typically maintains a global state that persists across navigation events.

This global state may include user authentication status, user preferences, shopping cart contents, and other data relevant to the application's functionality.

To manage this global state, SPAs often use state management libraries like Redux, Mobx, or context APIs provided by JavaScript frameworks.

These libraries enable developers to create and maintain a centralized state that can be accessed and modified from any component within the application.

For example, in a Redux-based SPA, you can define actions and reducers to update and retrieve the global state:

javascriptCopy code

```
// Define an action to update the user's authentication status const loginAction = (user) =>
({ type: 'LOGIN', payload: user, }); // Define a reducer to handle the authentication state const authReducer = (state = null, action) => { switch
```

(action.type) { case 'LOGIN': return action.payload; default: return state; } }); // Create a Redux store with the authReducer const store = createStore(authReducer);

In this code, the **loginAction** action updates the authentication state, and the **authReducer** reducer handles the state changes.

By using Redux or similar state management solutions, SPAs can maintain a consistent application state as users navigate between pages.

Additionally, these libraries offer tools for connecting React components to the global state, ensuring that components always reflect the latest state changes.

When building SPAs, developers often need to handle various navigation scenarios, such as redirects, nested routes, and route guards.

Redirects are commonly used to direct users to a specific page when they access a particular URL.

For example, you might want to redirect users from "/login" to "/dashboard" after they successfully log in.

In React Router, you can achieve this using the **<Redirect>** component or by programmatically navigating to the new URL.

Nested routes involve rendering components within other components based on the URL's structure.

For instance, a dashboard page may have nested routes for different sections like "/dashboard/profile" and "/dashboard/settings."

React Router and other routing libraries provide mechanisms for defining and handling nested routes.

Route guards are used to control access to specific routes based on certain conditions.

For example, you may want to prevent unauthorized users from accessing a private "/dashboard" route.

Route guards can be implemented using middleware functions that check conditions before allowing navigation to occur.

By handling these navigation scenarios effectively, SPAs can provide a smooth and secure user experience.

Additionally, SPAs often implement features like lazy loading, which load components or modules only when they are needed.

Lazy loading reduces the initial load time of the application and improves performance, especially for larger applications with many components.

Most JavaScript frameworks and libraries offer tools and techniques for implementing lazy loading in SPAs.

To summarize, navigating between pages in single-page applications is a crucial aspect of web development that requires careful consideration and implementation.

SPAs use client-side routing, URL manipulation, and global state management to provide a seamless user experience.

Developers can leverage routing libraries and state management solutions to simplify the process and address various navigation scenarios.

With proper navigation handling, SPAs can deliver responsive and engaging web applications that rival traditional multi-page counterparts while providing the benefits of dynamic content updates and a smooth user experience.

Chapter 8: Consuming APIs and Working with External Data

Processing and displaying external data is a fundamental task in modern web development, as web applications often rely on data from various sources to provide dynamic and up-to-date content.

External data can come from a wide range of origins, including APIs, databases, third-party services, and more.

Effectively retrieving, processing, and displaying this data is crucial for creating interactive and data-driven web applications.

Next, we will explore the techniques and best practices for handling external data in web development.

One of the most common ways to obtain external data is through APIs (Application Programming Interfaces).

APIs are used to request and exchange data between different software systems, and they have become a standard method for accessing data over the internet.

To interact with APIs, web developers often use JavaScript and libraries or frameworks like Axios, Fetch API, or jQuery's AJAX.

Here's an example of using Axios, a popular HTTP client for JavaScript, to make a GET request to an API and retrieve data:

```javascript
javascriptCopy code
const axios = require('axios');
axios.get('https://api.example.com/data')
.then((response) => { // Handle the API response
data const data = response.data; console.log(data);
}) .catch((error) => { // Handle errors
console.error(error); });
```

In this code, Axios is used to send a GET request to the "https://api.example.com/data" URL, and the API response data is processed in the **then** block.

APIs can return data in various formats, including JSON, XML, HTML, or plain text.

JSON (JavaScript Object Notation) is a commonly used format for data exchange due to its simplicity and compatibility with JavaScript.

Once the data is obtained from the API, it can be parsed and processed to extract the information needed for the web application.

For instance, if the API response is in JSON format, JavaScript's **JSON.parse()** method can be used to convert the JSON data into a JavaScript object that can be easily manipulated.

Another way to fetch external data is by using the Fetch API, which is built into modern web browsers and provides a native way to make HTTP requests.

Here's an example of using the Fetch API to retrieve data from an API:

javascriptCopy code

```
fetch('https://api.example.com/data')
.then((response) => response.json()) .then((data)
=> { // Handle the JSON data  console.log(data); })
.catch((error)    =>    {    //    Handle    errors
console.error(error); });
```

In this code, the Fetch API is used to make a GET request to the API URL.

The response is processed as JSON data in the second **then** block.

Using the Fetch API is a powerful and efficient way to fetch external data, especially when targeting modern web browsers.

Additionally, when working with external data, it's essential to handle errors gracefully.

Network issues, API changes, and other factors can lead to unsuccessful requests or unexpected data formats.

By using the **.catch()** block or handling errors within the promise chain, you can provide informative feedback to users and ensure that your application remains robust.

Beyond APIs, web developers often need to access data stored in databases.

Databases are used to store structured data, and web applications interact with them through database management systems (DBMS) like MySQL, PostgreSQL, MongoDB, or Firebase Realtime Database.

To retrieve data from databases, developers use server-side code and technologies.

Commonly, a server is responsible for querying the database and returning the requested data to the client-side application.

For example, in a Node.js application, you can use the **mysql** library to connect to a MySQL database and retrieve data:

javascriptCopy code

```javascript
const mysql = require('mysql'); const connection = mysql.createConnection({ host: 'localhost', user: 'username', password: 'password', database: 'mydatabase', }); connection.connect(); const query = 'SELECT * FROM mytable'; connection.query(query, (error, results) => { if (error) { console.error(error); return; } // Handle database query results console.log(results); }); connection.end();
```

In this code, a connection to a MySQL database is established, and a SQL query is executed to retrieve data from a table.

The retrieved data is then processed and used as needed within the application. When dealing with external data, it's crucial to consider data security and access control. APIs and databases often require authentication and authorization to protect sensitive data and ensure that only authorized users or applications can access it.

Authentication mechanisms like API keys, OAuth, or token-based authentication are commonly used to secure access to APIs.

Database systems, on the other hand, have their authentication and access control mechanisms.

For example, databases may require username and password authentication, and administrators can define user roles and permissions to control access to specific data and operations.

When working with external data, it's important to adhere to the security best practices recommended by the data provider or database system to ensure the confidentiality and integrity of the data.

Once external data is obtained, the next step is to display it within the web application's user interface.

This involves rendering the data in a format that is understandable and user-friendly.

Web developers often use HTML, CSS, and JavaScript to create dynamic and responsive data displays.

HTML is used to structure the content, while CSS is employed for styling and layout.

JavaScript adds interactivity and allows for dynamic updates based on user interactions or changes in the external data.

For instance, when displaying a list of items retrieved from an API, developers can use JavaScript to iterate through the data and generate HTML elements to represent each item.

Additionally, libraries and frameworks like React, Angular, and Vue.js provide tools for efficiently rendering external data and managing the user interface.

These libraries offer components and templates that can be bound to external data, making it easier to display and update information in real-time.

To illustrate, here's an example of rendering a list of items using React:

javascriptCopy code

```javascript
import React, { useState, useEffect } from 'react';
function App() { const [items, setItems] = useState([]); useEffect(() => { // Fetch external data and update 'items' state
fetch('https://api.example.com/items')
.then((response) => response.json()) .then((data) => setItems(data)) .catch((error) => console.error(error)); }, []); return ( <div> <h1>List of Items</h1> <ul> {items.map((item) => ( <li key={item.id}>{item.name}</li> ))} </ul> </div> ); }
export default App;
```

In this React example, the **useState** and **useEffect** hooks are used to manage the state of the items retrieved from an API.

The fetched data is mapped to HTML list items, creating a dynamic list of items displayed in the user interface.

Additionally, developers often implement features such as sorting, filtering, and pagination to enhance the user's ability to interact with external data.

These features can be achieved by using JavaScript libraries or custom code to manipulate and present the data effectively.

In summary, processing and displaying external data is a core aspect of web development that involves retrieving data from APIs, databases, or other sources and presenting it within a web application's user interface.

Developers use JavaScript and libraries or frameworks to interact with external data, ensuring proper error handling, security, and user-friendly displays.

By effectively managing and presenting external data, web applications can provide valuable and dynamic content to users, enhancing their experience and engagement.

Chapter 9: Responsive Design and Mobile Optimization

Making your web application mobile-friendly is essential in today's digital landscape, where an increasing number of users access websites and web apps from mobile devices such as smartphones and tablets.

Mobile-friendliness is not merely a matter of aesthetic design; it impacts the usability, accessibility, and overall success of your web application.

Next, we will explore the key principles and techniques for ensuring that your web application provides an optimal experience on mobile devices.

Responsive web design is a foundational concept in creating mobile-friendly web applications.

Responsive design is an approach that uses CSS media queries and flexible layout grids to adapt the layout and content of a web page to different screen sizes and resolutions.

By employing responsive design techniques, your web application can automatically adjust its appearance and functionality to suit the specific characteristics of mobile devices.

Media queries are CSS rules that define styles for different screen sizes or device orientations.

For example, you can use a media query to specify that certain CSS styles should apply only when the screen width is below a certain threshold, typically referred to as a "breakpoint."

Here's an example of a simple media query that changes the font size for screens with a maximum width of 600 pixels:

cssCopy code

```
@media screen and (max-width: 600px) { body {
font-size: 16px; } }
```

In this code, when the screen width is 600 pixels or less, the font size for the **body** element is set to 16 pixels.

By using media queries strategically throughout your CSS, you can create a responsive layout that adapts to various device sizes.

Flexible layout grids are another essential component of responsive web design.

Instead of relying on fixed-width layouts, flexible grids use relative units like percentages or viewport units to define the width of elements.

This flexibility allows elements to expand or contract based on the available screen space, ensuring that your web application's content remains readable and accessible on both large desktop monitors and small mobile screens.

CSS frameworks like Bootstrap and Foundation provide pre-built responsive grids that you can incorporate into your web application's layout.

These frameworks offer a set of CSS classes that make it easier to create responsive designs without having to write extensive custom CSS.

Here's an example of using Bootstrap's grid system to create a responsive layout:

htmlCopy code

```
<div class="container"> <div class="row"> <div class="col-md-6">Content on the left</div> <div class="col-md-6">Content on the right</div> </div> </div>
```

In this code, the **container**, **row**, and **col-md-6** classes are part of Bootstrap's grid system, and they help create a responsive two-column layout.

While responsive design plays a significant role in mobile-friendliness, it's just the beginning.

Ensuring that your web application is accessible and usable on mobile devices also involves considerations related to touch interactions, navigation, and performance.

Mobile devices primarily rely on touchscreens for user input, which differ significantly from traditional mouse and keyboard interactions.

To make your web application touch-friendly, you should ensure that interactive elements like buttons and links are appropriately sized and spaced to accommodate touch gestures.

Buttons and links should have a minimum touch target size to avoid accidental clicks, typically around 48x48 pixels or more.

Additionally, you should provide visual feedback when users interact with touch elements, such as highlighting buttons when tapped.

cssCopy code

```css
/* CSS to provide a visual touch feedback for buttons */ .button { padding: 10px; background-color: #007bff; color: #fff; border: none; cursor: pointer; transition: background-color 0.2s; } .button:hover { background-color: #0056b3; }
```

In this CSS example, the button element changes its background color when hovered, providing visual feedback to the user.

Mobile-friendly navigation is critical for ensuring that users can find their way around your web application on small screens.

On mobile devices, screen real estate is limited, so it's essential to design efficient navigation menus and structures.

Common mobile navigation patterns include using a collapsible navigation menu (hamburger menu), tabbed navigation, or a bottom navigation bar.

Let's take a look at an example of a simple collapsible navigation menu using HTML, CSS, and JavaScript:

htmlCopy code

```html
<!DOCTYPE html> <html lang="en"> <head> <meta charset="UTF-8"> <meta name="viewport" content="width=device-width, initial-scale=1.0"> <link rel="stylesheet" href="styles.css"> <script src="script.js"></script> <title>Mobile-Friendly Navigation</title> </head> <body> <header> <button id="menu-button"> ☰ </button> <nav id="nav-menu"> <ul> <li><a href="#">Home</a></li> <li><a
```

href="#">About</a></li>   <li><a
href="#">Services</a></li>   <li><a
href="#">Contact</a></li> </ul> </nav> </header>
</body> </html>

In this code, a button with the "☰" symbol represents the collapsible menu icon.

JavaScript is used to toggle the visibility of the navigation menu when the button is clicked.

javascriptCopy code

```javascript
// JavaScript to toggle the navigation menu const
menuButton = document.getElementById('menu-
button'); const navMenu =
document.getElementById('nav-menu');
menuButton.addEventListener('click', () => {
navMenu.classList.toggle('active'); });
```

The JavaScript code adds and removes the "active" class to toggle the visibility of the navigation menu.

By implementing mobile-friendly navigation patterns like this, you can enhance the user experience on small screens.

Performance optimization is another crucial aspect of mobile-friendliness.

Mobile devices often have slower network connections and less processing power than desktop computers.

To ensure that your web application loads quickly and performs well on mobile devices, you should follow performance best practices.

One key performance optimization is minimizing the size of web assets, such as images, scripts, and stylesheets.

You can use tools like image compressors, minification, and code splitting to reduce the size of these assets.

Additionally, enabling browser caching and utilizing content delivery networks (CDNs) can help improve load times.

Here's an example of enabling browser caching using HTTP headers in a server configuration:

bashCopy code

```
# Apache .htaccess example <IfModule mod_expires.c> ExpiresActive On ExpiresByType image/jpeg "access plus 1 year" ExpiresByType image/png "access plus 1 year" ExpiresByType text/css "access plus 1 year" ExpiresByType application/javascript "access plus 1 year" </IfModule>
```

In this example, the Apache web server is configured to set expiration dates for different types of assets, allowing browsers to cache them for a specified period.

Optimizing images is a critical aspect of performance. You can use image compression tools to reduce the file size of images without compromising quality.

For example, the ImageMagick command-line tool allows you to compress images efficiently:

graphqlCopy code

```
# Command to compress an image using
ImageMagick convert input.jpg -strip -interlace Plane
-quality 80% output.jpg
```

In this command, the input image "input.jpg" is compressed, and the resulting compressed image is saved as "output.jpg" with a reduced file size.

Performance monitoring and testing tools like Google PageSpeed Insights, Lighthouse, and GTmetrix can help identify performance bottlenecks and suggest optimizations for your web application.

By regularly assessing and improving your web application's performance, you can ensure that it loads quickly and runs smoothly on mobile devices, improving the overall user experience.

Accessibility is another critical aspect of mobile-friendliness. Web content accessibility guidelines (WCAG) provide standards and recommendations for making web content accessible to all users, including those with disabilities. Mobile devices are commonly used by people with disabilities, so it's crucial to design your web application with accessibility in mind.

Key accessibility considerations include providing descriptive text for images and interactive elements, ensuring keyboard navigation is possible, and offering alternative text for non-text content.

Here's an example of adding descriptive text to an image using the **alt** attribute:

htmlCopy code

```
<img src="example.jpg" alt="A person hiking in the
mountains">
```

In this code, the "alt" attribute provides a text description of the image's content, making it accessible to users with visual impairments who rely on screen readers.

Another critical aspect of accessibility is ensuring that form elements and interactive components are keyboard accessible.

Users with disabilities may rely on keyboard navigation or assistive technologies like screen readers, so your web application should allow them to interact with all elements without relying solely on a mouse or touch gestures.

Incorporating ARIA (Accessible Rich Internet Applications) attributes can further enhance the accessibility of complex widgets and interactive elements.

Testing your web application with accessibility evaluation tools and conducting usability testing with users of various abilities can help identify and address accessibility issues.

In summary, making your web application mobile-friendly involves adopting responsive web design principles, optimizing for touch interactions, implementing efficient navigation patterns, optimizing performance, and ensuring accessibility.

By following these guidelines and continuously testing your web application on mobile devices, you can provide a seamless and inclusive user experience for all your users, regardless of the devices they use.

Chapter 10: Deploying and Scaling TypeScript Web Applications

Scaling your web application for high traffic is a crucial consideration as your user base grows and the demand for your services increases.

Scaling involves expanding your application's infrastructure and optimizing its architecture to handle a larger volume of requests and concurrent users.

Next, we will explore various strategies and techniques for scaling your web application to ensure it remains performant and reliable under heavy loads.

One of the initial steps in preparing your web application for high traffic is to assess its current performance and identify potential bottlenecks.

You can use monitoring tools and performance profiling to gain insights into your application's behavior and resource utilization.

For example, tools like New Relic, Datadog, and Apache JMeter can help you collect performance data, analyze it, and identify areas that require optimization.

By understanding your application's performance characteristics, you can make informed decisions about which scaling strategies to implement.

Horizontal scaling, often referred to as "scaling out," involves adding more servers or instances to your application's infrastructure to distribute the incoming traffic and workload.

This approach can help improve both performance and fault tolerance.

To implement horizontal scaling, you can provision additional virtual machines or containers and deploy your application across multiple instances.

Container orchestration platforms like Kubernetes and Docker Swarm are commonly used to manage and scale containerized applications automatically.

For example, using Kubernetes, you can deploy multiple instances of your application as pods and configure load balancing to distribute incoming requests evenly among them.

bashCopy code

```
# CLI command to scale a Kubernetes deployment to
3 replicas kubectl scale deployment my-app-
deployment --replicas=3
```

In this command, the **kubectl scale** command is used to scale a Kubernetes deployment named "my-app-deployment" to three replicas, effectively increasing the application's capacity.

Another horizontal scaling technique is the use of content delivery networks (CDNs) to distribute static assets and cache content geographically.

CDNs have a network of edge servers located worldwide, which can reduce the latency for users accessing your web application from various regions.

By offloading static asset delivery to a CDN, your origin server can focus on handling dynamic content and application logic, leading to improved performance and reduced server load.

When designing your web application for horizontal scaling, consider stateless architecture, where each server instance does not store user-specific data.

User sessions and data should be stored externally, such as in a database or cache, allowing any server instance to handle a request from any user.

Vertical scaling, also known as "scaling up," involves increasing the capacity of individual server instances by adding more resources, such as CPU, RAM, or storage.

This approach can be suitable for applications that have a well-defined resource bottleneck, such as CPU-bound processes.

To vertically scale a server, you can resize its virtual machine or add more resources, either by upgrading the hardware or allocating additional resources to the cloud instance.

bashCopy code

```
# CLI command to resize a virtual machine in a cloud provider gcloud compute instances resize my-instance --machine-type=n1-standard-4
```

In this example, the **gcloud compute instances resize** command is used to change the machine type of a Google Cloud virtual machine to "n1-standard-4," which provides more CPU and RAM resources.

Caching is an effective technique for improving the performance and scalability of web applications.

Caches store frequently accessed data in memory or a fast storage layer, reducing the need to query databases or compute complex calculations for every request.

Popular caching solutions include Redis, Memcached, and CDNs.

Redis, for instance, can be used as an in-memory data store for caching frequently used database queries or computed results.

bashCopy code

```
# CLI command to install and start Redis server sudo apt-get install redis-server sudo systemctl start redis
```

In this example, the commands show how to install and start the Redis server on a Linux-based system using APT package manager and systemd.

To integrate Redis caching into your web application, you can use client libraries or middleware specific to your programming language or framework.

Implementing caching strategies like caching database query results, session data, or full page content can significantly reduce the load on your application's backend resources.

Load balancing is another essential technique for distributing incoming traffic across multiple server instances, ensuring that no single server becomes overwhelmed.

Load balancers act as intermediaries between clients and backend servers, forwarding requests to the appropriate server based on various algorithms or rules.

Popular load balancing solutions include HAProxy, NGINX, and cloud-based load balancers offered by major cloud providers.

For example, here's how to configure NGINX as a load balancer to distribute incoming requests to two backend server instances:

nginxCopy code

NGINX configuration for load balancing http { upstream backend { server backend-server-1; server backend-server-2; } server { listen 80; location / { proxy_pass http://backend; } } }

In this NGINX configuration, the **upstream** block defines two backend server instances, and the **proxy_pass** directive forwards incoming requests to them in a round-robin fashion.

When one server is under heavy load or experiencing issues, the load balancer can automatically redirect traffic to healthy servers, ensuring high availability and reliability.

Auto-scaling, also known as elastic scaling, is a dynamic scaling approach that automatically adjusts the number of server instances based on real-time traffic and workload.

Cloud providers like Amazon Web Services (AWS), Google Cloud Platform (GCP), and Microsoft Azure offer auto-scaling features that allow you to define scaling policies and rules.

For example, in AWS, you can create an auto-scaling group that monitors the CPU utilization of your instances and adds or removes instances as needed.
bashCopy code
CLI command to create an auto-scaling group in AWS aws autoscaling create-auto-scaling-group --auto-scaling-group-name my-group --launch-configuration-name my-launch-config --min-size 2 --max-size 10 --desired-capacity 2

In this AWS CLI command, an auto-scaling group named "my-group" is created with a minimum of two instances, a maximum of ten instances, and an initial desired capacity of two.

Auto-scaling helps your web application adapt to traffic spikes and seasonal variations while minimizing costs during periods of lower demand.

Database scaling is often a critical consideration when scaling your web application.

As traffic increases, database performance can become a bottleneck.

Horizontal database scaling involves distributing the database workload across multiple database servers or shards.

Sharding is a technique where data is divided into smaller, more manageable pieces, and each shard is stored on a separate database server.

Sharding can be implemented at the application level, where your application code determines which shard to query based on certain criteria, such as user IDs or geographical regions.

Alternatively, some database management systems offer built-in sharding capabilities.

For example, in MongoDB, you can configure sharding to distribute data across multiple servers using the **shardCollection** command:

bashCopy code

CLI command to enable sharding on a MongoDB collection   mongosh> sh.shardCollection("mydb.myCollection", { _id: "hashed" })

In this MongoDB command, the **sh.shardCollection** command is used to enable sharding on the "myCollection" collection using a hashed sharding key.

Database caching is another technique to enhance database performance and scalability.

Caching frequently accessed database queries or results in memory can reduce the need to hit the database for every request.

You can use caching layers like Redis or Memcached to store database query results temporarily.

pythonCopy code

Python code to cache database query results using Redis import redis import psycopg2 # Connect to Redis cache = redis.Redis(host='localhost', port=6379, db=0) # Check if the query result is in the cache cached_result = cache.get('my_query_result')

```
if cached_result is None: # Query the database conn
=               psycopg2.connect(database='mydb',
user='myuser',          password='mypassword',
host='localhost', port='5432') cur = conn.cursor()
cur.execute('SELECT * FROM mytable') result =
cur.fetchall() # Store the result in the cache for 1 hour
cache.setex('my_query_result', 3600, result) else: #
Use the cached result result = cached_result #
Process and return the result
```

In this Python example, Redis is used to cache the results of a database query, and the cached result is retrieved and used if available.

Database indexing and query optimization are crucial for database performance, especially as the data volume grows.

Ensure that your database is appropriately indexed to speed up common query operations.

Monitor slow queries and use database profiling tools to identify and optimize slow-performing queries.

Load testing is an essential part of preparing your web application for high traffic.

Load tests simulate heavy user traffic to assess how your application behaves under stress.

Tools like Apache JMeter, LoadRunner, and artillery can help you conduct load testing.

For example, to perform a load test with Apache JMeter, you can create a test plan that defines various user scenarios and configure the number of virtual users, ramp-up times, and test duration.

bashCopy code

```bash
# CLI command to run an Apache JMeter test plan
jmeter -n -t my_test_plan.jmx -l test_results.jtl
```

In this command, the **jmeter** CLI is used to execute a test plan defined in "my_test_plan.jmx" and save the results to "test_results.jtl."

Load tests can help you identify performance bottlenecks, server resource limits, and potential issues that may arise under heavy traffic conditions.

Content delivery networks (CDNs) play a crucial role in improving the scalability and performance of web applications, especially for serving static assets.

CDNs have a network of edge servers located in various geographical regions, allowing them to deliver content from a server that is physically closer to the user.

When a user requests static assets like images, stylesheets, or JavaScript files, the CDN automatically serves them from the nearest edge server, reducing latency and improving load times.

To leverage a CDN, you typically need to configure your web application to use it as the origin server for static assets.

CDN providers offer various integration methods and provide instructions on how to set up and configure your CDN service.

Content delivery networks also offer DDoS (Distributed Denial of Service) protection and security features to help safeguard your web application against attacks.

In summary, scaling your web application for high traffic involves a combination of strategies and techniques, including horizontal and vertical scaling, caching, load balancing, auto-scaling, database scaling, and load testing.

By carefully assessing your application's performance, addressing bottlenecks, and implementing the appropriate scaling solutions, you can ensure that your web application remains responsive and reliable even as user demand grows.

BOOK 4
TYPESCRIPT MASTERY
EXPERT-LEVEL TECHNIQUES: OPTIMIZING
PERFORMANCE AND CRAFTING COMPLEX
APPLICATIONS

ROB BOTWRIGHT

Chapter 1: Advanced TypeScript Language Features

In TypeScript, the type system offers a wide range of advanced features that allow developers to express complex relationships between types and ensure more robust code.

One such feature is "Union Types," which enables a variable to have multiple possible types.

For example, you can define a function that takes either a string or a number as an argument using a union type:

typescriptCopy code

```
function processInput(input: string | number): void
{ // Code that can handle both string and number
inputs }
```

In this case, the **input** parameter can accept either a string or a number value.

TypeScript also provides "Intersection Types," which allow you to combine multiple types into a single type.

For instance, you can create a type representing an object that has both "name" and "age" properties using an intersection type:

typescriptCopy code

```
type Person = { name: string; } & { age: number; };
```

The resulting **Person** type will require objects to have both "name" and "age" properties.

Another advanced type system feature is "Type Aliases," which allow you to create custom names for existing types, making your code more readable and maintainable.

typescriptCopy code

type Point = { x: number; y: number; }; function calculateDistance(pointA: Point, pointB: Point): number { // Calculate distance between two points }

Here, the **Point** type alias simplifies the function signature and makes it clear that **calculateDistance** expects two objects with "x" and "y" properties.

TypeScript's "Mapped Types" enable you to iterate over the properties of an existing type and create a new type based on those properties.

For example, you can transform all properties of an object type to be optional using a mapped type:

typescriptCopy code

type MakePropertiesOptional<T> = { [K in keyof T]?: T[K]; }; type PartialPerson = MakePropertiesOptional<Person>;

The **MakePropertiesOptional** mapped type turns every property of **Person** into an optional property, resulting in a type where all properties can be undefined.

Conditional Types are another powerful feature that allows you to create types based on conditions.

For instance, you can create a conditional type that checks if a given type is an array and returns the element type if true:

typescriptCopy code

```typescript
type ArrayElementType<T> = T extends (infer U)[] ? U : never; type ElementType = ArrayElementType<number[]>; // ElementType is number
```

In this example, the **ArrayElementType** conditional type checks if the type **T** is an array and, if so, infers the element type; otherwise, it returns **never**.

TypeScript's "Index Signatures" enable you to define objects with dynamic keys and their corresponding value types.

typescriptCopy code

```typescript
interface Dictionary { [key: string]: number; } const ages: Dictionary = { alice: 30, bob: 25, };
```

In this case, the **Dictionary** interface allows objects with string keys and values of type number.

Another advanced type feature is "Mapped Type Modifiers," which allow you to modify existing mapped types to create variations.

For example, you can create a mapped type that makes all properties of an object type read-only:

typescriptCopy code

```typescript
type Readonly<T> = { readonly [K in keyof T]: T[K]; };
type ImmutablePerson = Readonly<Person>;
```

The **Readonly** mapped type ensures that all properties of **ImmutablePerson** cannot be modified once they are set.

TypeScript also provides "Polymorphic this Types," which allow you to create methods in classes that return a new instance of the class, making method chaining fluent and type-safe.

typescriptCopy code

```typescript
class FluentCalculator { constructor(private value: number) {} add(num: number): this { this.value += num; return this; } subtract(num: number): this { this.value -= num; return this; } getValue(): number { return this.value; } } const result = new FluentCalculator(10).add(5).subtract(2).getValue(); // result is 13
```

The **this** type within the methods indicates that the methods return a new instance of the same class, allowing for method chaining.

Conditional "Mapped Types" are advanced type constructs that enable you to create complex mappings based on conditional logic.

You can use conditional mapped types to transform one type into another depending on specific conditions.

typescriptCopy code

```typescript
type StringifyIfString<T> = T extends string ? string : T; type TransformedTypes = StringifyIfString<number | string | boolean>;
```

In this example, the **StringifyIfString** conditional mapped type transforms the union type **number | string | boolean** into **string | number | boolean**, where only string types are changed to string.

The **keyof** keyword in TypeScript is a powerful tool for working with object types.

It allows you to extract the keys of an object type as a union of string literal types.

For example, if you have an object type like this:

typescriptCopy code

```
type Person = { name: string; age: number; };
```

You can use **keyof** to obtain the keys "name" and "age" as string literal types:

typescriptCopy code

```
type Keys = keyof Person; // Keys is "name" | "age"
```

This can be helpful for various tasks, such as creating mapped types, enforcing strict type checking, and creating dynamic property access.

TypeScript's "Mapped Types" allow you to create new types by transforming the properties of existing types. A common use case is to create a "Partial" mapped type, which makes all properties of an object type optional.

Here's how you can define a "Partial" mapped type:

typescriptCopy code

```
type Partial<T> = { [K in keyof T]?: T[K]; };
```

With this definition, you can make any object type partial by applying the "Partial" mapped type:

typescriptCopy code

```
type Person = { name: string; age: number; }; type
PartialPerson = Partial<Person>; const
partialPerson: PartialPerson = {}; // Valid
```

In this example, **Partial<Person>** transforms the **Person** type into a type where all properties are optional.

TypeScript's "Conditional Types" provide a way to create types that depend on conditions and runtime values.

You can use conditional types to express complex type logic based on the shape of types and their relationships.

Here's an example of a conditional type that checks if a type **T** is an array and returns its element type or returns the original type if not an array:

typescriptCopy code

```
type ArrayElementType<T> = T extends (infer U)[] ?
U : T; type ElementType =
ArrayElementType<number[]>; // ElementType is
number
```

In this case, the **ArrayElementType** conditional type checks if the type **T** extends **(infer U)[]**, which represents an array type.

If it does, it infers the element type **U**; otherwise, it returns the original type **T**.

Conditional types are versatile and can be used to create custom type transformations and constraints based on your specific needs.

TypeScript's "Type Inference" is a fundamental feature that allows the type checker to automatically deduce the type of a variable or expression based on its value.

242

This feature makes TypeScript's static typing powerful yet flexible.

Consider the following example:

typescriptCopy code

```
const message = "Hello, TypeScript!";
```

In this case, TypeScript automatically infers the type of the **message** variable as **string** because it is initialized with a string value.

Type inference works not only with simple types like strings but also with more complex types and even function return types:

typescriptCopy code

```
function add(a: number, b: number) { return a + b; }
const result = add(5, 3);
```

Here, TypeScript infers the return type of the **add** function as **number** because it detects that the function returns the result of adding two numbers.

Type inference is a crucial aspect of TypeScript that helps catch type-related errors at compile time while minimizing the need for explicit type annotations.

TypeScript's "Generics" feature allows you to write flexible and reusable code by creating functions, classes, and interfaces that can work with different data types.

Generics are similar to function parameters, but they represent types rather than values.

Consider the following example of a generic function that swaps the positions of two elements in an array:

typescriptCopy code

```typescript
function swap<T>(arr: T[], i: number, j: number):
void { const temp = arr[i]; arr[i] = arr[j]; arr[j] = temp;
} const numbers = [1, 2, 3, 4]; swap(numbers, 0,
2);
```

In this example, the **swap** function is generic because it can work with arrays of various data types, such as numbers, strings, or custom objects.

The **<T>** syntax inside the function's signature indicates that **T** is a type parameter that represents the array's element type.

Generics provide type safety while allowing you to write versatile and reusable code components.

TypeScript's "Type Guards" are a powerful tool for dealing with union types and narrowing down the possible types of a variable within a specific block of code.

Type guards are often used with conditional statements and allow you to perform type-specific operations based on runtime checks.

Here's an example of a type guard function that checks if a value is a string:

typescriptCopy code

```typescript
function isString(value: any): value is string { return
typeof value === "string"; } const data: unknown[]
= ["Hello", 42, true]; for (const item of data) { if
(isString(item)) { console.log(item.toUpperCase()); }
}
```

In this code, the **isString** function is a type guard that returns **true** if the **value** is a string.

Inside the loop, the **isString** type guard is used to narrow down the type of **item**, allowing you to safely call **toUpperCase** on string values.

TypeScript's "Type Assertions" provide a way to tell the type checker that you know the actual type of a value, even when the type checker cannot infer it.

Type assertions are useful when you have more knowledge about the shape and type of a value than TypeScript can determine statically.

Here's an example of a type assertion using the **<Type>** syntax:

typescriptCopy code

```
const value: unknown = "Hello, TypeScript!"; const length = (value as string).length;
```

In this code, the type assertion **(value as string)** tells TypeScript to treat **value** as a string, allowing you to access its **length** property.

While type assertions can be helpful in specific situations, it's essential to use them with caution and ensure that you're not introducing type-related errors.

TypeScript's "Type Compatibility" or "Type Inference" is a core feature that enables you to use values of one type as if they were another, as long as the types are compatible.

Type compatibility in TypeScript is based on a structural type system, meaning that types are considered compatible if their structures match, regardless of whether they have the same name or were declared separately.

For example, consider two interfaces with similar structures:

typescriptCopy code

```
interface Point2D { x: number; y: number; }
interface Point3D { x: number; y: number; z: number; } const point2D: Point2D = { x: 1, y: 2 };
const point3D: Point3D = point2D; // Compatible because the structure matches
```

In this example, the **point2D** object can be assigned to the **point3D** variable because their structures match, even though they have different interface types.

Type compatibility in TypeScript allows you to write more flexible and reusable code by focusing on the shape and structure of types rather than their names.

TypeScript's "Declaration Merging" is a feature that allows you to extend or combine multiple type or interface declarations with the same name into a single declaration.

This feature is especially useful when working with external libraries or modules that provide their own type definitions.

Consider a scenario where you want to extend the functionality of an existing interface:

typescriptCopy code

interface Person { name: string; } interface Person { age: number; } const person: Person = { name: "Alice", age: 30, };

In this example, TypeScript automatically merges the two **Person** interface declarations into one, resulting in an interface that has both **name** and **age** properties.

Declaration merging allows you to augment or extend existing types without the need to modify the original declarations, making it easier to work with third-party libraries and frameworks.

TypeScript's "Ambient Declarations" are a way to declare types for external libraries or modules that don't provide their own type definitions.

Ambient declarations let you tell TypeScript about the types and structures used in JavaScript libraries and ensure type safety when using them in your code.

You can declare ambient types in **.d.ts** files or using the **declare** keyword in a TypeScript file.

For example, to declare the type of a global variable provided by an external library:

typescriptCopy code

declare const myLibraryGlobal: any;

This tells TypeScript that there is a global variable **myLibraryGlobal** of type **any** from the external library.

You can also declare ambient modules to describe the shape of external modules:

typescriptCopy code

```
declare module "my-library" { export function
greet(name: string): string; }
```

In this example, an ambient module declaration for the "my-library" module provides type information for the **greet** function.

Ambient declarations are a powerful tool for ensuring type safety when working with JavaScript libraries that lack native TypeScript support.

TypeScript's "Type Utility" functions, introduced in TypeScript 2.8 and later, provide a set of built-in utility types for manipulating and transforming existing types.

These utility types allow you to create new types by applying transformations to existing types, making it easier to work with complex type manipulations.

Here are some commonly used utility types:

Partial\<T>: Makes all properties of a type **T** optional.

Required\<T>: Makes all properties of a type **T** required.

Readonly\<T>: Makes all properties of a type **T** read-only.

Record\<K, T>: Creates a type with specified keys **K** and values of type **T**.

Pick\<T, K>: Picks a subset of properties from type **T** by specifying keys **K**.

Omit\<T, K>: Omits a subset of properties from type **T** by specifying keys **K**.

Exclude\<T, U>: Excludes types from type **T** that are assignable to type **U**.

Extract<T, U>: Extracts types from type **T** that are assignable to type **U**.

NonNullable<T>: Removes **null** and **undefined** from type **T**.

These utility types provide a concise way to manipulate and create new types, reducing the need for custom type declarations and improving code maintainability.

TypeScript's "Decorators" are a powerful feature that allows you to add metadata and behavior to classes, methods, properties, and parameters.

Decorators are typically used in conjunction with classes and provide a way to annotate and enhance their functionality.

Here's an example of a simple class decorator:

typescriptCopy code

```
function logClassName(target: any) { console.log(`Class name: ${target.name}`); } @logClassName class MyClass { // Class implementation } // Output: Class name: MyClass
```

In this example, the **@logClassName** decorator logs the name of the class when it is defined.

Decorators can also be applied to methods, properties, and parameters, and they can be used to modify behavior, validate inputs, or add custom logic to a class.

TypeScript's decorators are widely used in frameworks like Angular and libraries like MobX to provide additional functionality and declarative annotations to classes and their members.

TypeScript's "Modules" feature allows you to organize your code into reusable and maintainable units by encapsulating related functionality into separate files and exposing parts of it as needed.

Modules help you manage the complexity of larger codebases and improve code organization, making it easier to understand and maintain your projects.

In TypeScript, you can use the **import** and **export** keywords to work with modules.

Here's an example of exporting a function from one module and importing it into another:

typescriptCopy code

```
// math.ts (module 1) export function add(a: number, b: number): number { return a + b; } // app.ts (module 2) import { add } from "./math"; const result = add(5, 3); // Result is 8
```

In this example, the **add** function is exported from the "math.ts" module and imported into the "app.ts" module.

You can also use module aliases to simplify imports:

typescriptCopy code

```
// math.ts (module 1) export function add(a: number, b: number): number { return a + b; } // app.ts (module 2) import * as math from "./math"; const result = math.add(5, 3); // Result is 8
```

TypeScript supports various module formats, including CommonJS, AMD, ES6 modules, and more, making it flexible for different environments and workflows.

TypeScript's "Namespace" is a way to group related code and types under a single global name, preventing naming conflicts and providing organization within your codebase.

Namespaces are especially useful when working with external libraries or when you want to create a structured hierarchy in your code.

Here's an example of defining a namespace and using it to encapsulate code:

typescriptCopy code

```
// Shapes.ts (namespace) namespace Shapes {
export class Circle { constructor(public radius:
number) {} area(): number { return Math.PI *
this.radius ** 2; } } export class Rectangle {
constructor(public width: number, public height:
number) {} area(): number { return this.width *
this.height; } } } // app.ts const circle = new
Shapes.Circle(5); console.log(circle.area()); //
Output: 78.54 const rectangle = new
Shapes.Rectangle(4,                              6);
console.log(rectangle.area()); // Output: 24
```

In this example, the **Shapes** namespace encapsulates the **Circle** and **Rectangle** classes, preventing naming conflicts and providing a clear structure.

Namespaces in TypeScript are a useful tool for organizing and structuring your code, especially when working with larger projects or external libraries.

TypeScript's "Type Definition Files" (d.ts) are a way to provide type information for JavaScript libraries and modules that were not originally written in TypeScript.

These declaration files allow you to use TypeScript's static type checking and IntelliSense features when working with external JavaScript code.

Declaration files typically have the extension **.d.ts** and contain type annotations for the APIs and types defined in the corresponding JavaScript code.

Here's an example of a simple declaration file for a JavaScript library:

typescriptCopy code

```
// jquery.d.ts declare var $: { (selector: string): any; ajax(url: string, settings?: any): void; };
```

In this declaration file, the **$** variable is declared with type information for its functions and properties.

Once you have a declaration file in your TypeScript project, you can use the library as if it were written in TypeScript:

typescriptCopy code

```
// app.ts $("button").click(function () { // TypeScript provides type information for jQuery functions alert("Button clicked!"); });
```

TypeScript's support for declaration files allows you to work seamlessly with popular JavaScript libraries and leverage the benefits of static typing and tooling.

TypeScript's "Type Inference" is a powerful feature that enables the type checker to automatically deduce the type of a variable or expression based on its value.

This feature makes TypeScript's static typing powerful yet flexible.

Consider the following example:

typescriptCopy code

```typescript
const message = "Hello, TypeScript!";
```

In this case, TypeScript automatically infers the type of the **message** variable as **string** because it is initialized with a string value.

Type inference works not only with simple types like strings but also with more complex types and even function return types:

typescriptCopy code

```typescript
function add(a: number, b: number) { return a + b; }
const result = add(5, 3);
```

Here, TypeScript infers the return type of the **add** function as **number** because it detects that the function returns the result of adding two numbers.

Type inference is a crucial aspect of TypeScript that helps catch type-related errors at compile time while minimizing the need for explicit type annotations.

TypeScript's "Generics" feature allows you to write flexible and reusable code by creating functions, classes, and interfaces that can work with different data types.

Generics are similar to function parameters, but they represent types rather than values.

Consider the following example of a generic function that swaps the positions of two elements in an array:

typescriptCopy code

```
function swap<T>(arr: T[], i: number, j: number): void { const temp = arr[i]; arr[i] = arr[j]; arr[j] = temp; } const numbers = [1, 2, 3, 4]; swap(numbers, 0, 2);
```

In this example, the **swap** function is generic because it can work with arrays of various data types, such as numbers, strings, or custom objects.

The **<T>** syntax inside the function's signature indicates that **T** is a type parameter that represents the array's element type.

Generics provide type safety while allowing you to write versatile and reusable code components.

TypeScript's "Type Guards" are a powerful tool for dealing with union types and narrowing down the possible types of a variable within a specific block of code.

Type guards are often used with conditional statements and allow you to perform type-specific operations based on runtime checks.

Here's an example of a type guard function that checks if a value is a string:

typescriptCopy code

```
function isString(value: any): value is string { return
typeof value === "string"; } const data: unknown[]
= ["Hello", 42, true]; for (const item of data) { if
(isString(item)) { console.log(item.toUpperCase()); }
}
```

In this code, the **isString** function is a type guard that returns **true** if the **value** is a string.

Inside the loop, the **isString** type guard is used to narrow down the type of **item**, allowing you to safely call **toUpperCase** on string values.

TypeScript's "Type Assertions" provide a way to tell the type checker that you know the actual type of a value, even when the type checker cannot infer it.

Type assertions are useful when you have more knowledge about the shape and type of a value than TypeScript can determine statically.

Here's an example of a type assertion using the **<Type>** syntax:

typescriptCopy code

```
const value: unknown = "Hello, TypeScript!"; const
length = (value as string).length;
```

In this code, the type assertion **(value as string)** tells TypeScript to treat **value** as a string, allowing you to access its **length** property.

While type assertions can be helpful in specific situations, it's essential to use them with caution and ensure that you're not introducing type-related errors.

TypeScript's "Type Compatibility" or "Type Inference" is a core feature that enables you to use values of one type as if they were another, as long as the types are compatible.

Type compatibility in TypeScript is based on a structural type system, meaning that types are considered compatible if their structures match, regardless of whether they have the same name or were declared separately.

For example, consider two interfaces with similar structures:

typescriptCopy code

```
interface Point2D { x: number; y: number; }
interface Point3D { x: number; y: number; z: number; } const point2D: Point2D = { x: 1, y: 2 };
const point3D: Point3D = point2D; // Compatible because the structure matches
```

In this example, the **point2D** object can be assigned to the **point3D** variable because their structures match, even though they have different interface types.

Type compatibility in TypeScript allows you to write more flexible and reusable code by focusing on the shape and structure of types rather than their names.

TypeScript's "Declaration Merging" is a feature that allows you to extend or combine multiple type or interface declarations with the same name into a single declaration.

This feature is especially useful when working with external libraries or modules that provide their own type definitions.

Consider a scenario where you want to extend the functionality of an existing interface:

typescriptCopy code

interface Person { name: string; } interface Person { age: number; } const person: Person = { name: "Alice", age: 30, };

In this example, TypeScript automatically merges the two **Person** interface declarations into one, resulting in an interface that has both **name** and **age** properties.

Declaration merging allows you to augment or extend existing types without the need to modify the original declarations, making it easier to work with third-party libraries and frameworks.

TypeScript's "Ambient Declarations" are a way to declare types for external libraries or modules that don't provide their own type definitions.

Ambient declarations let you tell TypeScript about the types and structures used in JavaScript libraries and ensure type safety when using them in your code.

You can declare ambient types in **.d.ts** files or using the **declare** keyword in a TypeScript file.

For example, to declare the type of a global variable provided by an external library:

typescriptCopy code
declare const myLibraryGlobal: any;

This tells TypeScript that there is a global variable **myLibraryGlobal** of type **any** from the external library.

Chapter 2: Performance Optimization Strategies

Profiling and identifying performance bottlenecks in your software applications is a crucial aspect of optimizing their performance.

One powerful tool for profiling and identifying bottlenecks is the Chrome DevTools. To use it, open Google Chrome and navigate to the webpage you want to profile.

Press **F12** or right-click on the page and select "Inspect" to open the DevTools. In the DevTools, go to the "Performance" tab.

Click the circular record button to start profiling, then perform the actions or interactions in your web application that you want to analyze.

Once done, stop profiling by clicking the stop button. The DevTools will display a timeline of events, showing you what happened during the profiling session.

You can identify bottlenecks by looking for spikes in the timeline, which indicate areas of your code or the web page that are consuming excessive resources or causing slowdowns.

Another profiling technique involves using JavaScript profilers, like the **console.time** and **console.timeEnd** functions.

These functions allow you to measure the time it takes for specific code blocks to execute. You can insert them into your code to create timestamps before and after the code you want to profile:

javascriptCopy code

```
console.time("MyFunction"); // Code to profile
console.timeEnd("MyFunction");
```

This technique is helpful for pinpointing which parts of your code are taking the most time to execute.

Additionally, you can use Node.js's built-in profiler by running your application with the **--inspect** flag.

This will enable the Chrome DevTools to connect to your Node.js application, allowing you to profile server-side code.

To use it, run your Node.js application with the following command:

bashCopy code

```
node --inspect your-app.js
```

Then, open Chrome and go to **chrome://inspect** to access the DevTools for your Node.js application.

In addition to profiling, identifying bottlenecks requires understanding common performance pitfalls. One common bottleneck is excessive DOM manipulation. Frequent updates to the DOM can slow down web applications significantly.

To mitigate this, consider batching DOM updates, using libraries like React or Vue.js for efficient rendering, or utilizing virtual DOM techniques.

Another bottleneck is network requests. Excessive or large network requests can lead to slow page load times.

Optimize by minimizing the number of requests, compressing data, and using a Content Delivery Network (CDN) for static assets.

Database queries can also be a bottleneck, especially in server-side applications.

Use proper indexing, caching, and query optimization techniques to improve database performance.

Inefficient algorithms and data structures can cause bottlenecks as well.

Review your code to ensure that you're using appropriate data structures and algorithms for the tasks at hand.

Memory leaks can also lead to performance issues over time.

Use tools like Chrome DevTools' Memory tab or Node.js's **--inspect** flag to identify and fix memory leaks in your applications.

Consider load testing your application to simulate high traffic conditions and identify performance bottlenecks under stress.

Tools like Apache JMeter or artillery.io can help with load testing.

When you identify a bottleneck, it's essential to profile and gather data to understand the root cause fully.

Profiling tools will give you insights into where your code is spending the most time and consuming the most resources.

Once you've identified a performance bottleneck, prioritize addressing it based on its impact on the user experience and the complexity of the fix.

Remember that not all bottlenecks are equal, and some may have a more significant impact on performance than others.

Regularly monitoring and profiling your application is essential for maintaining optimal performance, as performance bottlenecks can emerge over time due to changes in code, data, or user behavior.

In summary, profiling and identifying performance bottlenecks is a critical part of software optimization.

Using tools like Chrome DevTools, JavaScript profilers, and Node.js's built-in profiler, along with understanding common performance pitfalls, will help you pinpoint and address bottlenecks effectively.

By continuously monitoring and optimizing your code, you can ensure that your applications provide the best possible user experience.

Chapter 3: Advanced Design Patterns in TypeScript

The Singleton and Factory patterns are two widely used design patterns in software development, and they can be effectively implemented in TypeScript to enhance the structure and maintainability of your code.

The Singleton pattern is used to ensure that a class has only one instance, and it provides a global point of access to that instance. In TypeScript, you can create a Singleton class using a private constructor and a static method to retrieve the instance:

typescriptCopy code

```
class Singleton { private static instance: Singleton;
private constructor() { // Private constructor to
prevent instantiation } public static getInstance():
Singleton { if (!Singleton.instance) {
Singleton.instance = new Singleton(); } return
Singleton.instance; } public someMethod(): void {
// Implement Singleton's functionality here } } const
singleton1 = Singleton.getInstance(); const
singleton2 = Singleton.getInstance();
console.log(singleton1 === singleton2); // true, as
they reference the same instance
```

In this example, the **Singleton** class ensures that there is only one instance by controlling the instantiation process. When you call **Singleton.getInstance()**, it either creates a new instance or returns the existing one.

The Factory pattern, on the other hand, is a creational design pattern used for creating objects without specifying the exact class of object that will be created. It defines an interface for creating an object but allows subclasses to alter the type of objects that will be created. TypeScript makes it easy to implement the Factory pattern using class inheritance:

typescriptCopy code

```typescript
abstract class Product { abstract getDescription(): string; } class ConcreteProductA extends Product { getDescription(): string { return 'Product A'; } } class ConcreteProductB extends Product { getDescription(): string { return 'Product B'; } } class Factory { createProduct(type: string): Product { switch (type) { case 'A': return new ConcreteProductA(); case 'B': return new ConcreteProductB(); default: throw new Error('Invalid product type'); } } } const factory = new Factory(); const productA = factory.createProduct('A'); const productB = factory.createProduct('B');
console.log(productA.getDescription()); // 'Product A' console.log(productB.getDescription()); // 'Product B'
```

In this Factory pattern example, the **Factory** class is responsible for creating different types of **Product** objects based on the provided type. Subclasses like **ConcreteProductA** and **ConcreteProductB** implement the actual products. This decouples the client code from the specific product classes, making it more flexible and maintainable.

Both the Singleton and Factory patterns can be useful in various scenarios. The Singleton pattern is handy when you need a single point of control for a particular resource or configuration, while the Factory pattern excels in scenarios where object creation needs to be abstracted, and the specific class of objects may change over time.

In TypeScript, these patterns become even more powerful due to the type checking and static analysis it offers. This ensures that your Singleton instances are indeed singletons and that your Factory classes return the correct types of objects.

When deploying TypeScript code that incorporates these patterns, you follow the standard TypeScript compilation process. You use the TypeScript compiler (**tsc**) to transpile your TypeScript code into JavaScript, and then you can run the resulting JavaScript in your chosen runtime environment. Here's a simplified step-by-step guide to deploying TypeScript code:

Install TypeScript: If you haven't already, you can install TypeScript globally using npm:

bashCopy code

npm install -g typescript

Write Your TypeScript Code: Develop your Singleton and Factory patterns in TypeScript.

Compile TypeScript: Use the TypeScript compiler (**tsc**) to transpile your TypeScript code into JavaScript:

bashCopy code

```
tsc your-code.ts
```

This will generate a JavaScript file (**your-code.js**) that you can run in your environment.

Run the JavaScript Code: Execute your JavaScript code as you would with any other JavaScript application, whether it's in a Node.js environment or a web browser.

The TypeScript compiler ensures that your code adheres to the type annotations and correctness constraints, providing an added layer of assurance when deploying your patterns. It also helps catch potential issues during development, reducing the likelihood of runtime errors.

In summary, the Singleton and Factory patterns are valuable tools in software design, and TypeScript's strong typing and compilation process enhance their effectiveness. Incorporating these patterns into your TypeScript projects can lead to more organized and maintainable code. Deploying TypeScript code follows the standard compilation and execution process, ensuring that your patterns work as intended in your chosen runtime environment.

Chapter 4: Unit Testing and Test-Driven Development (TDD)

Test-Driven Development (TDD) is a software development methodology that places a strong emphasis on writing tests before writing the actual code.

The fundamental principle behind TDD is to write a failing test that specifies the desired behavior of a piece of code before implementing that behavior.

This approach helps developers gain confidence that their code works correctly and provides a safety net for refactoring and future changes.

In TDD, the development cycle typically follows three main steps: "Red," "Green," and "Refactor."

In the "Red" phase, you write a failing test case that describes the behavior you want to implement.

For example, if you're building a function that calculates the sum of two numbers, you might start with a test case that asserts the function returns the correct sum.

Here's an example of a failing test in TypeScript using a testing framework like Jest:

typescriptCopy code

```
test('adds 1 + 2 to equal 3', () => { expect(add(1, 2)).toBe(3); });
```

In this test, the **add** function has not been implemented yet, so the test fails.

The next step is the "Green" phase. In this phase, you write the minimum amount of code required to make the failing test pass.

For our example, you would implement the **add** function to return the correct sum:

typescriptCopy code

```typescript
function add(a: number, b: number): number {
return a + b; }
```

Now, when you run the test again, it should pass, indicating that the code meets the specified behavior.

The final step is the "Refactor" phase. In this phase, you can improve and optimize your code without changing its behavior, confident that your tests will catch any regressions.

TDD encourages writing small, focused tests that cover specific aspects of your code's behavior.

These tests serve as documentation for how your code is intended to work and provide a safety net against introducing bugs when making changes.

TDD also promotes writing tests that check for edge cases, boundary conditions, and error handling, helping to ensure robust and reliable software.

In addition to improving code quality, TDD can lead to several benefits, including increased developer confidence, faster development cycles, and easier debugging.

It encourages developers to think about their code's design and maintainability from the beginning, leading to cleaner and more maintainable codebases.

TDD can also help catch and fix issues early in the development process, reducing the cost of addressing defects later in the project.

While TDD offers many advantages, it's essential to understand its challenges and limitations.

Writing tests before code can initially slow down development, and it may require a mindset shift for developers accustomed to traditional development approaches.

Moreover, TDD may not be suitable for all projects, especially those with rapidly changing requirements or tight deadlines.

To implement TDD in TypeScript, you can choose from various testing frameworks such as Jest, Mocha, or Jasmine.

These frameworks provide tools and utilities for writing and running tests in TypeScript projects.

Here's a brief example of setting up a TypeScript project with Jest for TDD:

Initialize a TypeScript project:

bashCopy code

npm init -y

Install TypeScript and Jest:

bashCopy code

npm install --save-dev typescript jest @types/jest

Configure TypeScript:

Create a **tsconfig.json** file with your TypeScript configuration.

Create a test file:

Write your test cases in a **.test.ts** or **.spec.ts** file. For example, **myModule.test.ts**.

Write your code:

Implement the code in a TypeScript file, for example, **myModule.ts**.

Run tests:

Use the Jest test runner to execute your tests:

bashCopy code

npx jest

This setup enables you to practice TDD in your TypeScript project by writing failing tests, implementing code to make them pass, and refactoring as needed.

In summary, Test-Driven Development is a powerful methodology for building reliable, maintainable software.

It involves writing tests before implementing code, following the "Red-Green-Refactor" cycle, and using testing frameworks like Jest to automate the process in TypeScript projects.

While TDD can be initially challenging and may not suit every project, it offers numerous benefits, including improved code quality, early bug detection, and increased developer confidence.

Chapter 5: Building Scalable and Maintainable Codebases

Maintaining software code is a critical aspect of software development that often receives less attention than initial development but is equally if not more important in the long run.

Code maintainability refers to the ease with which you can modify, update, and extend your codebase without introducing errors or negatively impacting its performance.

Maintaining code can become increasingly challenging as a project grows in size and complexity, making it essential to follow best practices to ensure code remains manageable.

One fundamental best practice for code maintainability is writing clean, readable code.

Using meaningful variable and function names, following consistent formatting and indentation, and adding comments when necessary make it easier for you and other developers to understand the code.

Leveraging a version control system, such as Git, is another crucial aspect of code maintainability.

Git helps you track changes, collaborate with others, and revert to previous versions when needed, all of which are essential for maintaining code integrity.

Regularly reviewing and refactoring code is essential for keeping it maintainable.

Refactoring involves restructuring code to improve its readability, efficiency, and maintainability without changing its external behavior.

Automated testing plays a significant role in maintaining code quality.

By writing unit tests, integration tests, and end-to-end tests, you can ensure that code modifications do not introduce regressions or new bugs.

Continuous Integration (CI) and Continuous Deployment (CD) pipelines help maintain code quality by automatically building, testing, and deploying code changes. Tools like Jenkins, Travis CI, and GitHub Actions integrate seamlessly with version control systems to provide automated testing and deployment workflows.

Another best practice is documenting your code thoroughly. This includes writing API documentation, providing usage examples, and explaining design decisions. Well-documented code is easier to maintain and collaborate on.

Avoiding code duplication is crucial for code maintainability. Duplication increases the risk of inconsistencies and makes it harder to update code in multiple places. Use functions, classes, and modules to encapsulate reusable code.

Applying design patterns can improve code maintainability.

Design patterns offer proven solutions to common design problems and can make code more predictable and easier to extend.

When deploying code changes, consider using containerization technologies like Docker.

Docker allows you to package your application and its dependencies into a container, ensuring consistent environments in development, testing, and production.

Implementing versioning for APIs and libraries helps maintain compatibility with existing code that relies on them.

Semantic versioning (semver) is a popular versioning scheme that communicates the nature of changes through version numbers.

Code reviews are essential for maintaining code quality.

Peer reviews help catch issues early and ensure code adheres to coding standards and best practices.

Monitoring and logging are vital for understanding how your code performs in production.

Logging helps identify errors and performance bottlenecks, while monitoring allows you to track the health of your application.

Code maintainability also involves planning for security.

Implement security best practices, conduct regular security audits, and keep dependencies up-to-date to mitigate security risks.

In addition to these best practices, it's essential to foster a culture of code maintainability within your development team.

Encourage open communication, knowledge sharing, and the willingness to refactor and improve code continuously.

As for deploying changes to maintainable code, you should follow a structured process.

Before deploying, thoroughly test changes in a staging environment to catch any issues before they impact production.

Use version control tags or branches to keep track of deployed versions.

Consider using deployment automation tools like Ansible or Terraform to manage infrastructure as code, ensuring consistency across environments.

Rolling back to a previous version is another aspect of code maintainability.

Having a well-defined rollback plan and automated deployment procedures can simplify the process in case of issues.

Finally, ensure that your production environment is monitored closely.

Use tools like Prometheus, Grafana, or application-specific monitoring services to track performance and detect anomalies.

In summary, code maintainability is a vital aspect of software development that should not be overlooked.

By following best practices for clean code, version control, testing, documentation, and deployment, you can ensure that your code remains manageable and adaptable throughout its lifecycle.

Chapter 6: Advanced Error Handling and Debugging Techniques

Exception handling is a crucial aspect of developing robust and reliable applications. It involves handling unforeseen errors or exceptional situations gracefully to prevent application crashes or data corruption.

In modern software development, exception handling is an essential component of building robust and maintainable applications. By implementing effective exception handling strategies, you can improve the stability and reliability of your software.

One common approach to exception handling is using try-catch blocks. In languages like TypeScript, you can use try-catch blocks to wrap code that might throw exceptions, allowing you to handle errors gracefully. Here's an example:

typescriptCopy code

```
try { // Code that may throw an exception const
result = divide(10, 0); console.log(result); } catch
(error) { // Handle the exception console.error(`An
error occurred: ${error.message}`); }
```

In this example, if the **divide** function attempts to divide by zero, it throws an exception, which is caught and handled in the catch block.

It's essential to handle exceptions appropriately by providing clear error messages and taking appropriate actions. Depending on the nature of the error, you may choose to log the error, display a user-friendly message, or perform additional recovery actions.

Another key aspect of exception handling is using custom exceptions. While many programming languages provide built-in exceptions for common error scenarios, you can create custom exceptions to represent application-specific errors more effectively. Custom exceptions allow you to provide detailed information about the error and implement specific handling logic.

In TypeScript, you can define custom exceptions by extending the **Error** class. Here's an example:

typescriptCopy code

```
class CustomError extends Error { constructor(message: string) { super(message); this.name = 'CustomError'; } } try { // Code that may throw a custom exception throw new CustomError('This is a custom exception.'); } catch (error) { if (error instanceof CustomError) { // Handle the custom exception console.error(`Custom error occurred: ${error.message}`); } else { // Handle other exceptions console.error(`An error occurred: ${error.message}`); } }
```

By creating custom exceptions, you can differentiate between various error scenarios and handle them appropriately in your application.

Exception handling also involves proper logging and error reporting. Logging exceptions is essential for debugging and monitoring your application's behavior in production. You can use logging libraries like Winston or Pino in TypeScript to log exceptions to files or external services.

Additionally, consider implementing error reporting and monitoring tools such as Sentry or Rollbar to track exceptions in your application. These tools provide insights into the frequency and context of exceptions, helping you identify and address issues quickly.

When deploying an application with robust exception handling, you should ensure that error logs are accessible and that you have a mechanism in place to receive notifications or alerts when critical exceptions occur. These practices help you proactively address issues in your production environment.

Furthermore, consider implementing retry and fallback mechanisms in your application for scenarios where transient errors may occur. Retry logic can help mitigate the impact of temporary issues like network outages or database failures. Implementing fallback strategies ensures that your application can provide degraded but functional service when encountering unexpected errors.

Lastly, conduct thorough testing of your exception handling mechanisms. Write unit tests and integration tests to cover various error scenarios and edge cases. This helps you validate that your exception handling code behaves as expected and gracefully handles exceptions.

In summary, exception handling is a critical aspect of building robust and reliable applications. Effective exception handling strategies involve using try-catch blocks, creating custom exceptions, proper logging, error reporting, and implementing retry and fallback mechanisms. Deploying an application with robust exception handling requires monitoring, alerting, and thorough testing to ensure the stability and reliability of the software in production environments.

Chapter 7: Concurrency and Parallelism in TypeScript

Synchronizing asynchronous operations is a common challenge in modern software development. Asynchronous operations are essential for building responsive and efficient applications, but they can introduce complexity when multiple asynchronous tasks need to be coordinated or synchronized.

One common scenario where synchronization is required is making multiple asynchronous API calls and waiting for all of them to complete before proceeding with further processing.

In JavaScript and TypeScript, the most common approach to synchronizing asynchronous operations is to use Promises and the **async/await** syntax.

The **Promise.all** method allows you to execute multiple asynchronous operations concurrently and wait for all of them to complete. Here's an example:

```
typescriptCopy code
async function fetchData() { const [userData, postList] = await Promise.all([ fetchUserData(), fetchPosts(), ]); // Further processing using userData and postList }
```

In this example, the **fetchUserData** and **fetchPosts** functions are asynchronous and return Promises. By using **Promise.all**, both functions are called concurrently, and **await** ensures that the function continues only when both Promises have resolved.

Another approach for synchronizing asynchronous operations is the use of callbacks. Callbacks allow you to specify a function to be executed when an asynchronous operation completes. To synchronize multiple callbacks, you can use control flow libraries like Async.js or utilize the callback pattern itself.

Here's an example using callbacks:

typescriptCopy code

```
function fetchData(callback) {
fetchUserData((userDataError, userData) => { if
(userDataError) { callback(userDataError); return; }
fetchPosts((postError, postList) => { if (postError) {
callback(postError); return; } // Further processing
using userData and postList callback(null, { userData,
postList }); }); }); }
```

In this callback-based approach, we nest the asynchronous operations and handle errors along the way. Once both operations complete successfully, we invoke the **callback** with the results.

A different approach to synchronizing asynchronous operations is using the **async/await** syntax in combination with the **for...of** loop. This allows you to iterate over an array of Promises, awaiting each one sequentially.

typescriptCopy code

```
async function fetchData() { const promises =
[fetchUserData(), fetchPosts()]; const results = [];
for (const promise of promises) { results.push(await
promise); } // Further processing using results }
```

In this example, we create an array of Promises and iterate over them using **for...of**, awaiting each Promise to complete before moving to the next one. The results are stored in the **results** array, which can be used for further processing.

Additionally, you can employ asynchronous libraries like RxJS or use the built-in **async/await** capabilities of modern JavaScript/TypeScript to handle more complex synchronization scenarios, such as combining and merging asynchronous streams of data.

When deploying applications with synchronized asynchronous operations, it's crucial to test thoroughly. Ensure that your synchronization mechanisms work correctly under various conditions, including error scenarios and concurrency issues. Implement proper error handling and logging to detect and diagnose issues in production environments.

Furthermore, consider optimizing the performance of synchronized asynchronous operations. You can use techniques like parallelism, caching, and load balancing to improve the efficiency of your application.

In summary, synchronizing asynchronous operations is a common challenge in software development, but it can be effectively managed using Promises, **async/await**, callbacks, or control flow libraries. Thorough testing and optimization are essential to ensure that your synchronization mechanisms work reliably and efficiently in production environments.

Chapter 8: Working with Databases and APIs

Integrating and consuming external APIs is a fundamental aspect of modern software development, allowing applications to interact with external services, retrieve data, and perform various operations.

One common scenario in software development is accessing data or functionality provided by external web services through their APIs.

To integrate and consume external APIs effectively, developers need to understand the API's documentation and endpoints.

API documentation typically provides information about the available endpoints, request methods, authentication requirements, and expected response formats.

Once you have a clear understanding of the API, you can use various programming languages and libraries to make HTTP requests to the API's endpoints.

In JavaScript and TypeScript, the **fetch** API is commonly used to make HTTP requests. Here's an example of how to use it to fetch data from an external API:

typescriptCopy code

```
async function fetchData() { try { const response =
await fetch('https://api.example.com/data'); if
(!response.ok) { throw new Error('Network
```

response was not ok'); } const data = await response.json(); // Process and use the retrieved data } catch (error) { console.error('Error fetching data:', error); } }

In this example, we use the **fetch** function to send an HTTP GET request to the external API's endpoint. We check the response status, handle potential errors, and parse the response data as JSON.

Authentication is a crucial aspect of integrating with external APIs. Many APIs require authentication to ensure data security and access control.

Common authentication methods include API keys, OAuth tokens, and bearer tokens. The API documentation will specify the required authentication method and how to include authentication credentials in your requests.

Here's an example of using an API key for authentication:

typescriptCopy code

const apiKey = 'your-api-key'; async function fetchData() { try { const response = await fetch('https://api.example.com/data', { headers: { 'Authorization': `Bearer ${apiKey}`, }, }); // Handle the response as before } catch (error) { console.error('Error fetching data:', error); } }

When integrating with external APIs, it's important to handle rate limiting and pagination if the API imposes limits on the number of requests or paginates large data sets.

Rate limiting refers to restrictions on the number of requests you can make within a specific time frame. You should respect these limits to avoid being temporarily or permanently blocked from the API.

Pagination is relevant when an API returns large sets of data divided into smaller chunks (pages). You need to make multiple requests and follow pagination links to retrieve all the data.

Caching is another consideration when integrating with external APIs.

Caching can help reduce the load on the external service and improve the response time of your application. You can implement caching at various levels, including client-side caching and server-side caching.

When deploying applications that consume external APIs, it's crucial to monitor API usage and performance.

Implement logging and monitoring to keep track of the number of requests, response times, and error rates. This information can help you identify and address issues in real-time.

Scaling considerations also come into play when consuming external APIs.

As your application grows, you may need to scale your infrastructure to handle increased API traffic. Techniques like load balancing and horizontal scaling can be employed to distribute the load efficiently.

Lastly, it's important to stay informed about changes and updates to the external API.

API providers may release new versions, change authentication methods, or deprecate endpoints. Regularly check the API documentation and consider versioning your API integration to avoid disruptions.

In summary, integrating and consuming external APIs is a fundamental skill in modern software development.

Understanding API documentation, handling authentication, rate limiting, pagination, and caching, and monitoring API usage and performance are essential aspects of this process. Deploying applications that consume external APIs requires attention to scalability and staying informed about API changes to ensure smooth operation.

Chapter 9: Real-Time Applications and WebSockets

Implementing chat applications and collaboration tools is a complex and rewarding endeavor that allows individuals and teams to communicate, share information, and collaborate effectively in real-time.

These applications have become increasingly essential in today's world, enabling remote work, project collaboration, and seamless communication across geographical boundaries.

To create chat applications and collaboration tools, developers have several options in terms of technologies, frameworks, and libraries.

One popular choice for building real-time chat applications is to use WebSocket technology. WebSockets provide a full-duplex communication channel over a single TCP connection, allowing for real-time data exchange between clients and servers.

Node.js, a JavaScript runtime, is often used to implement WebSocket servers, thanks to its non-blocking I/O and event-driven architecture. To set up a WebSocket server in Node.js, you can use libraries like **ws**:

javascriptCopy code

```
const WebSocket = require('ws'); const wss = new WebSocket.Server({ port: 8080 }); wss.on('connection', (ws) => { console.log('Client
```

connected'); ws.on('message', (message) => {
console.log(`Received: ${message}`); // Handle
incoming messages and broadcast to other clients
wss.clients.forEach((client) => { if (client !== ws &&
client.readyState === WebSocket.OPEN) {
client.send(message); } }); }); ws.on('close', () => {
console.log('Client disconnected'); }); });

In this example, we create a WebSocket server using
the **ws** library, listen on port 8080, and handle
incoming connections, messages, and disconnections.

Client-side technologies like HTML, CSS, and
JavaScript (or frameworks like React or Angular) are
used to create the user interface for chat applications.
WebSocket libraries, such as **socket.io**, simplify client-
side WebSocket interactions.

Authentication and authorization are crucial aspects
of chat applications. You'll need to implement user
authentication to verify the identity of users and
ensure data security. Techniques like OAuth, JSON
Web Tokens (JWT), or custom authentication
mechanisms can be used.

To persist chat messages and data, databases are
employed. Popular choices include SQL databases like
PostgreSQL or NoSQL databases like MongoDB. Data
modeling and schema design depend on the specific
requirements of your application.

Security is a paramount concern when implementing
chat applications and collaboration tools. Protecting
user data, securing WebSocket connections, and

preventing common security vulnerabilities like Cross-Site Scripting (XSS) and Cross-Site Request Forgery (CSRF) are essential.

Deployment of chat applications can be done on cloud platforms like AWS, Azure, or Google Cloud. Using containerization technologies like Docker and container orchestration platforms like Kubernetes can simplify deployment and scaling.

For example, you can deploy a WebSocket server using Docker with the following command:

bashCopy code

```
docker run -d -p 8080:8080 my-websocket-server
```

This command runs a containerized WebSocket server on port 8080 in detached mode.

Scaling chat applications involves load balancing incoming WebSocket connections across multiple server instances to handle increased user loads. WebSocket load balancers like **nginx** or specialized WebSocket proxies can distribute traffic efficiently.

Real-time chat applications often require features like message history, notifications, file sharing, and user presence indicators. These features can be implemented using a combination of database queries, WebSocket events, and frontend components.

Testing chat applications and collaboration tools is essential to ensure that they function correctly under various scenarios, including multiple users, concurrent messaging, and error conditions.

Automated testing tools like Jest for unit testing and tools like Selenium or Puppeteer for end-to-end testing can be beneficial in this regard.

In summary, implementing chat applications and collaboration tools is a challenging but rewarding task in modern software development. Technologies like WebSockets, Node.js, client-side frameworks, and databases play crucial roles in creating real-time communication platforms. Security, authentication, deployment, scaling, and testing are essential considerations throughout the development process. Building feature-rich chat applications and collaboration tools can greatly enhance communication and collaboration within teams and across organizations.

Chapter 10: Building Large-Scale TypeScript Applications

Architecting large-scale TypeScript applications is a complex and crucial task that requires careful planning and design to ensure maintainability, scalability, and long-term success.

Large-scale applications typically have multiple modules, components, and layers of complexity, making it essential to establish a clear and robust architecture from the beginning.

One common architectural pattern for large-scale TypeScript applications is the Model-View-Controller (MVC) or Model-View-ViewModel (MVVM) pattern, which separates the application into distinct layers to manage data, presentation, and user interaction.

In TypeScript, building a scalable and maintainable application often involves using a modular approach. You can organize your codebase into separate modules or packages to encapsulate related functionality and maintain a clean and understandable code structure.

TypeScript's module system allows you to create reusable and isolated components, which can be essential in large-scale applications. You can use features like namespaces, modules, and import/export statements to structure your codebase effectively.

For instance, you can create separate modules for user authentication, data fetching, UI components, and business logic, and then import and use them as needed throughout your application.

Dependency management is a critical aspect of large-scale TypeScript applications. You can use a package manager like npm or yarn to manage external dependencies and keep your project's dependencies up-to-date.

To add a new dependency using npm, you can use the following CLI command:

bashCopy code

```
npm install package-name
```

This command installs the specified package and updates your project's **package.json** file.

It's essential to establish clear guidelines and best practices for code organization and naming conventions. Consistency in naming, folder structure, and coding style helps maintain a coherent codebase and simplifies collaboration among team members.

Using a TypeScript-aware IDE or code editor can significantly enhance your development experience when working on large-scale applications. IDEs like Visual Studio Code offer features such as intelligent code completion, type checking, and refactoring tools that streamline the development process.

When architecting large-scale TypeScript applications, you should consider the use of design patterns. Design patterns provide proven solutions to recurring design problems and help you create maintainable and robust code.

For example, the Singleton pattern ensures that a class has only one instance, which can be valuable for managing global application state in a large-scale application. You can implement the Singleton pattern in TypeScript like this:

typescriptCopy code

```
class Singleton { private static instance: Singleton;
private constructor() { // Initialize the Singleton }
public static getInstance(): Singleton { if
(!Singleton.instance) { Singleton.instance = new
Singleton(); } return Singleton.instance; } }
```

This pattern ensures that there's only one instance of the **Singleton** class throughout your application.

Another important consideration is testing. Large-scale TypeScript applications benefit from comprehensive testing to ensure that new features and changes don't introduce regressions. You can use testing frameworks like Jest or Mocha to write unit tests, integration tests, and end-to-end tests for your application.

To run tests using Jest, you can use the following CLI command:

bashCopy code

```
npm test
```

This command executes the tests defined in your project.

As your large-scale TypeScript application grows, you'll likely need to handle state management more effectively. Libraries like Redux or MobX can help you manage the application's state, especially when dealing with complex user interfaces and data flow.

Deploying a large-scale TypeScript application typically involves setting up a production environment on a server or a cloud platform. Deployment processes can vary depending on your project's requirements and infrastructure.

You can use platform-specific deployment tools or scripts to automate the deployment process. For example, deploying a Node.js application to a cloud platform like AWS can involve using tools like AWS Elastic Beanstalk or AWS Lambda.

In summary, architecting large-scale TypeScript applications is a multifaceted endeavor that requires careful planning, modularization, dependency management, coding conventions, design patterns, testing, and effective state management. TypeScript's features and ecosystem support the development of maintainable and scalable codebases. Additionally, using TypeScript-aware IDEs and following best practices can significantly enhance the development experience for large-scale projects.

Strategies for deployment and scalability are critical considerations when bringing your application to production and ensuring it can handle increased traffic and growing user demand.

Deploying a web application involves making it accessible to users over the internet. The deployment process can vary depending on your technology stack, infrastructure, and hosting provider.

One common approach to deploying web applications is to use cloud platforms like Amazon Web Services (AWS), Microsoft Azure, or Google Cloud Platform (GCP). These platforms offer scalable and flexible infrastructure services, making it easier to manage your application's deployment.

To deploy your application on AWS, for example, you can use the Elastic Beanstalk service, which simplifies the process of deploying and managing web applications.

Here's an example of deploying a Node.js application to AWS Elastic Beanstalk using the AWS CLI:

bashCopy code

```
eb init -p node.js my-app eb create my-app-env eb deploy
```

These commands initialize the Elastic Beanstalk environment, create an environment, and deploy your application to the cloud.

Containerization is another deployment strategy gaining popularity. Containers allow you to package your application and its dependencies into a single, lightweight unit that can run consistently across different environments.

Docker is a widely-used containerization platform that enables you to build, ship, and run containers. To deploy a Dockerized application, you can use container orchestration tools like Kubernetes or Docker Swarm.

Here's an example of deploying a Docker containerized application to Kubernetes:

bashCopy code

```
kubectl create deployment my-app --image=my-image:tag kubectl expose deployment my-app --port=80 --type=LoadBalancer
```

These commands create a deployment and expose it as a service with a load balancer.

Scalability is a crucial aspect of deploying web applications, especially if you anticipate increased traffic and user demand. There are two primary approaches to scaling: vertical scaling and horizontal scaling.

Vertical scaling involves increasing the resources (CPU, memory) of a single server or virtual machine to handle additional load. You can resize your server manually or automatically based on usage metrics.

Horizontal scaling, on the other hand, involves adding more servers or instances to distribute the load. Load balancers are used to evenly distribute incoming requests among multiple servers. Cloud providers offer auto-scaling features to dynamically add or remove instances based on demand.

When dealing with databases, scalability is a different challenge. Scaling a relational database can be complex, but cloud providers offer managed database services that handle scalability for you.

For example, Amazon RDS (Relational Database Service) automatically scales compute and storage resources based on your database's workload.

Caching is an effective strategy to improve application performance and reduce the load on your servers. Caching stores frequently accessed data in memory, making it faster to retrieve.

You can use tools like Redis or Memcached as in-memory data stores for caching. Middleware like Varnish or CDNs (Content Delivery Networks) can cache content at the edge, closer to the user, reducing latency.

Monitoring and observability are crucial for maintaining a healthy and performant application. You can use monitoring tools like Prometheus, Grafana, or application performance management (APM) services to gain insights into your application's behavior.

Set up alerts to notify you of any anomalies or issues, ensuring that you can react quickly to maintain uptime and performance.

Security is a top concern in deployment strategies. Implement security best practices, such as using HTTPS, securing sensitive data, and regularly patching and updating your software and dependencies.

Consider using Web Application Firewalls (WAFs) and intrusion detection systems (IDS) to protect against threats and attacks.

Finally, implement continuous integration and continuous deployment (CI/CD) pipelines to automate the testing, building, and deployment of your application. CI/CD pipelines ensure that changes are thoroughly tested and deployed consistently, reducing the risk of errors in production.

In summary, strategies for deployment and scalability are essential for ensuring your web application's success in a production environment. Consider cloud platforms, containerization, and scaling techniques to handle increased traffic and user demand effectively. Use caching, monitoring, security best practices, and CI/CD pipelines to optimize performance and maintain reliability.

Conclusion

In this comprehensive book bundle, "TypeScript Programming in Action: Code Editing for Software Engineers," we embarked on a journey through the world of TypeScript, from the fundamentals to the most advanced techniques. Across four meticulously crafted volumes, we explored TypeScript's power and versatility, equipping both beginners and seasoned developers with the knowledge and skills needed to excel in TypeScript programming.

In "Book 1 - TypeScript for Beginners," we provided a gentle yet thorough introduction to TypeScript, taking readers on a step-by-step journey through its core concepts and syntax. From understanding data types and variables to exploring essential programming constructs, we set a solid foundation for those new to TypeScript.

"Book 2 - Mastering TypeScript Essentials" then elevated our learning, delving into advanced concepts and practical applications tailored for intermediate developers. We tackled TypeScript's intricacies, explored complex data structures, and honed our skills in real-world scenarios, ensuring readers were well-equipped to tackle more challenging projects.

"Book 3 - TypeScript in Depth" took us on an exciting journey into web development with TypeScript. We ventured into the creation of web applications, applying TypeScript's capabilities to solve real-world problems. Through hands-on projects and examples, we gained a deeper understanding of how TypeScript can empower us in building robust and dynamic web solutions.

Finally, in "Book 4 - TypeScript Mastery," we reached the pinnacle of TypeScript expertise. This volume dived into expert-level techniques, optimizing performance, and crafting complex applications. We explored intricate topics, such as metaprogramming, dependency injection, and advanced design patterns, ensuring that readers could take on the most challenging software development tasks with confidence.

Throughout this book bundle, we emphasized practicality and real-world application. Each book was carefully structured to provide a well-rounded learning experience, complete with code examples, best practices, and valuable insights garnered from years of industry experience.

As we conclude this journey through TypeScript programming, it's essential to recognize that the world of software development is ever-evolving. TypeScript, with its robust type system and versatile capabilities, continues to play a significant role in shaping the future of web and application development.

Whether you are just beginning your TypeScript journey or have reached the level of mastery, the knowledge and skills gained from this book bundle will serve as valuable assets in your software engineering career. TypeScript's vibrant ecosystem and community provide endless opportunities for innovation and growth, and we encourage you to continue exploring and pushing the boundaries of what you can achieve with this remarkable language.

With this bundle, we hope to have equipped you with the tools, insights, and expertise needed to excel in TypeScript programming. Whether you're building web applications, optimizing performance, or crafting complex software solutions, TypeScript is your trusted companion on the path to software engineering excellence.

Thank you for embarking on this TypeScript adventure with us, and we wish you continued success in your coding endeavors. May your TypeScript programming skills continue to flourish and empower you to bring your software visions to life.

www.ingramcontent.com/pod-product-compliance
Lightning Source LLC
Chambersburg PA
CBHW070937050326
40689CB00014B/3239